RSS *for* Educators

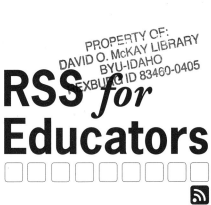

🔊 **Blogs, Newsfeeds,
Podcasts, and Wikis
in the Classroom**

John G. Hendron

International Society for Technology in Education
EUGENE, OREGON • WASHINGTON, DC

RSS *for* Educators

Blogs, Newsfeeds, Podcasts, and Wikis in the Classroom

John G. Hendron

Director of Book Publishing: Courtney Burkholder
Acquisitions Editor: Jeff V. Bolkan
Production Editor: Lynda Gansel
Production Coordinator: Maddelyn High
Graphic Designer: Signe Landin
Copy Editor: Tim A. Taylor
Cover/Book Design and Production: Lindsay Starr
Indexer: Seth Maslin, Potomac Indexing LLC

Library of Congress Cataloging-in-Publication Data

Hendron, John G.
  RSS for educators : blogs, newsfeeds, podcasts, and wikis in the classroom / John G.
Hendron. — 1st ed.
    p. cm.
  Includes bibliographical references and index.
  ISBN-13: 978-1-56484-239-8 (pbk.)
  1. Computer-assisted instruction. 2. Educational technology. 3. RSS feeds. I. Title.
  LB1028.5.H39 2008
  371.33'44678—dc22

                                                        2007048635

First Edition
ISBN: 978-1-56484-239-8

Printed in the United States of America

International Society for Technology in Education (ISTE)
Washington, DC, Office:
  1710 Rhode Island Ave. NW, Suite 900, Washington, DC 20036-3132
Eugene, Oregon, Office:
  175 West Broadway, Suite 300, Eugene, OR 97401-3003
Order Desk: 1.800.336.5191
Order Fax: 1.541.302.3778
Customer Service: orders@iste.org
Book Publishing: books@iste.org
Rights and Permissions: permissions@iste.org
Web: www.iste.org

ABOUT ISTE

The International Society for Technology in Education (ISTE) is the trusted source for professional development, knowledge generation, advocacy, and leadership for innovation. A nonprofit membership association, ISTE provides leadership and service to improve teaching, learning, and school leadership by advancing the effective use of technology in PK–12 and teacher education.

Home of the National Educational Technology Standards (NETS), the Center for Applied Research in Educational Technology (CARET), and the National Educational Computing Conference (NECC), ISTE represents more than 85,000 professionals worldwide. We support our members with information, networking opportunities, and guidance as they face the challenge of transforming education. To find out more about these and other ISTE initiatives, visit our Web site at **www.iste.org**.

As part of our mission, ISTE Book Publishing works with experienced educators to develop and produce practical resources for classroom teachers, teacher educators, and technology leaders. Every manuscript we select for publication is carefully peer-reviewed and professionally edited. We look for content that emphasizes the effective use of technology where it can make a difference—increasing the productivity of teachers and administrators; helping students with unique learning styles, abilities, or backgrounds; collecting and using data for decision making at the school and district levels; and creating dynamic, project-based learning environments that engage today's learners. We value your feedback on this book and other ISTE products. E-mail us at **books@iste.org**.

ABOUT THE AUTHOR

 John G. Hendron is a graduate of the University of Rochester, where he studied music at the Eastman School and anthropology and Spanish at the university's College of Arts, Sciences, and Engineering. He became an accomplished conductor while pursuing graduate studies at Case Western Reserve University and performing with the University Circle Wind Ensemble at the Cleveland Institute of Music. Most recently, John earned a second graduate degree from Virginia Tech. His interests include gourmet cookery, photography, video editing, and baroque music. He has been employed since 1999 as a teacher and instructional technologist for Goochland County Public Schools in Virginia, and he freelances as a graphic and Web designer. In December, 2006, he received the Virginia State Technology Leadership Award from the Virginia Department of Education. He can be found online at **www.johnhendron.net**.

CONTENTS

I have been using computers for as long as I can remember. Growing up in the 1980s, I was fortunate to have access to computers in schools and at home, when programming had become a hobby. I was among a generation of those who not only turned in their middle-school writing assignments in the form of a print-out from a dot matrix printer, but who were also (like my friends and I) composing text on their computers. For many, the entire writing process became computer-based, despite this being a foreign way of doing things to our teachers. With this early exposure to computers, it should be no surprise that today I find myself passionately exploring emerging and exciting technologies. My own professional quest over the past eight years has been to explore how technology can make a difference in the lives of students and teachers.

My professional life has placed me in front of both educators and K–12 students. I love the school environment. For anyone involved in the educational environment, the learning never stops. When I work with teachers in the role of an advocate or as a trainer, I am sometimes told, "Well, this stuff is easy for you. You're the computer guy. I'll never get this!" First, I remind them about the importance of why we are spending time together. "This technology is a part of the lives of your students," I say. "It's a big and growing part of their culture. If we're to reach students, we need to be conversant with that culture in a number of ways." Teachers are usually interested in what I've said, but often still doubtful that technology can help them.

Then I remind them, "Remember, I was a music teacher. I wasn't born with microchips in my head. Technology is for everyone!" My own enthusiasm for technology and the effects it now has on our lives typically carries us along during training.

During teacher training, there's never enough time to cover everything in sufficient detail for everyone. That's one of the reasons I decided to write this book—so readers can take their time learning about a set of technologies that are already making a significant impact in the way we teach and the ways our students learn.

Over the past eight years, teachers have witnessed some very positive outcomes using computers in their schools. I have highlighted some of these throughout the book. The changes in pedagogy introduced in our schools are due in large part to trust among colleagues, a willingness to have fun, and a duty to help every one of our students succeed. I am indebted to many for the support I have received from colleagues in our local consortia, including the Greater Richmond Area Education Technology Council (GRAETC); from state-wide organizations, such as the Virginia Society for Technology in Education (VSTE); and especially indebted to our local technology team in Goochland County, Virginia (www.glnd.k12.va.us), including my supervisor Mr. Thomas DeWeerd and my colleagues and partners, Mr. Peter Martin, Mrs. Jennifer Bocrie, and Mr. Sean Campbell. Sharing a common vision and respect for one another, in addition to enjoying one's own profession, has been a rewarding experience for all of us.

My second reason for writing this book is to share what I know—both the expertise and the mistakes—with you, the reader. You are in a position to begin using these new tools and technologies today to begin expanding your professional toolset.

This book is for anyone who is interested in making sense of how to use an emerging class of World Wide Web-based technologies. It is for educators who know there is something new ahead. It is for administrators and teachers who want to make an impact on the ways their students are learning and communicating. For those of you responsible for (or involved with) staff development, this book aims to provide the *whys* and *hows* of using podcasts, Web syndication, weblogs, wikis, and more. It's also for those of you who have heard terms like *Web 2.0, wiki,* and *RSS* and want to know what the buzz is all about.

Welcome to the New Web

A NEW ERA

A powerful technology, but a simple concept, Really Simple Syndication (RSS) makes it possible to easily access frequently updated content on the Internet. Rather than checking your favorite Web site every day to see if any new content is available, RSS enables you to "subscribe" and have updated content automatically delivered to your computer. RSS is widely used in connection with blogging and podcasting. This chapter will illustrate the concepts surrounding RSS, weblogs (or blogs), and podcasts, and will explain why these technologies are so valuable to educators and their students.

First, a brief history. In the late fall of 2004, a new delivery method for obtaining multimedia content over the Internet gained momentum. The folks who began exchanging audio and video files in this new way called the method "podcasting." Using RSS, people began to subscribe to their favorite podcasts and have the audio or video content automatically delivered to their computer or portable media player. The advent of podcasting might be seen as a turning point, a single point in time when enough people got together, used available technologies, and created a new class of communication. This behavior, we will see, is typical of netizens during this new Web era. We might even look at things historically as "pre-podcast" and "post-podcast."

Around the same time that podcasting was born, we began to see the emergence of a new class of Web sites, one that enabled us to do things we could never do before. On these Web sites, we could interact with one another, and we could manipulate content easily, without having to know HTML or other programming. For example, on some sites we could post pictures or video and tag them according to our own categories. This was a paradigm shift, and many are calling this new breed of the World Wide Web "Web 2.0." This new Web version enables us not only to read content that others have written and published on a server, but it also lets us easily take part in the act of publishing ourselves. Web 2.0 has also been called the "Read/Write Web."

Whichever term you apply to this new breed of technologies, and no matter which technologies you may or may not have already used, we are going to explore them and their impact on how we do business in schools. For those of you new to Read/Write tools, these new technologies enable people to evolve beyond being mere consumers of online content. More people are able to collaborate, share, and communicate online because the technology behind the Read/Write Web is easy to use.

MAKING SENSE OF RSS AND READ/WRITE TECHNOLOGIES

RSS

Really Simple Syndication is a popular method for subscribing to new content that is published online. (You will see this written elsewhere as "Web syndication," and this term embraces all formats of this idea, including another format of syndication called "Atom.")

Here is how RSS works. Say you have a Web site where you publish lecture notes every day after class. In the so-called Web 1.0 framework, your students need to visit your Web site on a regular basis, check to see that you have updated your site, find the new lecture notes, and then download them. This method works great as long as you are consistent in posting—and as long as your students are dutiful in retrieving—lecture notes each evening after class.

Using Web syndication, you post your new Web page of lecture notes, but you also publish a second file to your Web server. This file is known by many names: "newsfeed file," "XML file," "RSS file," and there are likely others. This file is basically a catalog of all your lecture notes. Your students, in turn, have installed a new type of application on their computers called a "newsreader" or "news aggregator." This program has one function: it checks a Web server and downloads an identified RSS newsfeed file on a regular basis (e.g., once a day or once an hour).

The news aggregator is not unlike your e-mail program, which effectively (and continually) asks the server, "Is there new mail?" When the news aggregator compares the newsfeed file on the server to a previously accessed version and sees that an update has been made, it alerts your students ("Hey! A new lecture has been posted!"). It will even download the lecture notes for your students. You can think of this news aggregator as a little robot that is regularly in touch with your server, continually asking it, "Anything new yet? … How about now?" When the server reports new content, the aggregator dutifully downloads it and waits for more.

When we find a Web site that is using RSS, we call the process of adding the syndication file to your news aggregator a "subscription." You might tell your students, "Tonight, you can subscribe to my lecture notes," and as long as your students are subscribed, your notes will be on their computers waiting to be read.

Some teachers I've talked with have worries about Web syndication. They hear the term "subscription" and think they will have to pay for this service. Rest assured that subscriptions, like most of what I cover in this book, are free. When you are subscribed to a Web site, RSS is simply the syndication technology that performs the background checks across the Web—from your computer to a server somewhere else—continually checking for new content.

Weblog (Blog)

Weblogs started out humbly enough in the second half of the 1990s and helped ignite the popularity of the Read/Write Web. Historically, I think we will look at the eight-year period between 1996 (when the first weblogs began to emerge) and 2004 (when podcasting emerged) as the transitional years between Web 1.0 and Web 2.0.

So what is a weblog, or blog? The *web* part of the word is easy. But *log?* Some see weblogs as diaries; others as journals. Blogs often provide news, observations, or commentary on a subject. The entries in a blog are called "posts," and they typically appear in a list in reverse chronological order, with the newest posts at the top. A person who writes or maintains a blog is called a "blogger." Bloggers write in all kinds of different ways. You can find blogs on practically any topic. Some bloggers write their posts as long essays, and others write short, brief updates. Whatever content or style the blog utilizes, it often includes links and images in addition to the text. A blog is one of the easiest ways to put content on the Web.

While studying music in college, I began blogging by posting reviews of music recordings online. I next turned-on several teachers to blogging simply as a means to get content easily on the Web for their students to use. "This is so easy!" I heard. Compared to authoring a Web page with HTML or a visual editor, publishing via a blog is simple.

At around the same time, podcasting quietly emerged, and the blogging phenomenon gained cultural status through the prism of politics. Many Americans were introduced to blogs through the evening news' reports of so-called political bloggers who, for example, were critical of United States Senator Trent Lott, or who were critical or supportive of news anchor Dan Rather's reporting. Democrat Howard Dean made waves by using blogs and the talents of grass-roots advocates to raise money via the Web.

Blogs are easily and frequently updated Web pages that anyone, regardless of technical prowess, can maintain. Authoring a blog can be a solo or group pursuit, and it can be done inexpensively. The best blogs are frequently updated, satisfying a reader's desire for something new.

Blogs today are set apart from other types of Web sites through several attributes. First, many blogs enable readers to add comments to individual posts. Second, blogs have a list of links to other blogs and sites of interest, called a "blogroll." Third, blogs many times contain links to individual posts, called "permalinks." Last, some blogs include the ability to link to other blog posts by different authors, called a "trackback."

Podcasts

Podcasts are often likened to radio shows. Podcasting is firmly rooted in the concept of Web syndication: you subscribe to a podcast in the same way you can subscribe to an RSS feed on a Web site. The difference is what you are subscribing to. Instead of text, such as lecture notes, a podcast can be an audio or video file. RSS is at play in the background, automatically grabbing new media from another Web server.

What happens if you are an emerging band and want an audience for your music? There's the traditional route of demo tapes, record deals, and airplay on radio stations. But what if we could use the Internet to better attract the public's ears and wallets?

The earliest podcasts were born in this way—multimedia files of music tracks from unknown artists, or broadcasts by folks who thought, for example, they had talent talking about politics, the news, or whatever crossed their minds. These files were not, however, podcasts *yet*. The creators of these media files began to use blog software to publish their content through what has become known as "videoblogs" and "audioblogs."

Dave Winer, who is a well-known blogger, and Adam Curry, known best for his video DJ gig on MTV in the 1980s, helped propel the podcast concept. Many folks found audio content online through simple downloads and audioblogs, and then transferred this content to their portable music players. Winer and Curry began evangelizing a way to find audio content and push it to you over the latest version of RSS. This new RSS 2.0 format enabled content creators to embed a multimedia attachment in the RSS newsfeed file that anyone could publish to a Web server. New software was required to subscribe to so-called podcast feeds. These were nothing more than RSS news-feeds that included the audio. The software downloaded these audio files and saved them locally on our hard drives. Even newer software did something else: it copied the content to our iPods—at the time, the most popular portable audio player.

At first, podcasting was dominated by well-known names. But once people learned how to subscribe to a podcast and copy the content over to their portable players, they soon wanted to create their own podcasts. The popularity of podcasting only helped benefit Apple Computer, creator of the iPod. Today, their iTunes software is one of the easiest ways to subscribe to podcasts and to transfer both the audio and video variants to Apple's own iPods. With the advent of podcasting, the Read/Write Web was no longer limited to text.

Wikis

Finally, we get to wikis—the strange, and perhaps even exotic-sounding Web technology. Wikis are likely older than both podcasts and blogs. The name *wiki* is borrowed from the Hawaiian *wiki-wiki*, which means "quick" or "fast." Wikis might be thought of as "quick and dirty" Web pages. But wait—didn't we just say that blogs were easy-to-create Web pages? Both wikis and blogs are, in fact, easy means to getting content published online, but their format and purpose differ.

Remember that blogs are made up of short, individual posts of content. Each chunk of information you publish online through a blog has a nice one-to-one relationship to a "newsitem" in a newsfeed. In blogs, the most recent content is listed first in a long list of content. If this content, to use our earlier example, is lecture notes, the most recent lecture notes would appear at the top of the blog.

A wiki is a type of Web site that enables different users to publish documents and create links between documents, all within the familiar confines of a regular Web browser. While blogs are made up of posts, the model for content in a wiki is the more common "document," or Web page, no matter how long or short. Perhaps one of the best examples of a wiki is the free online encyclopedia, Wikipedia. Each page translates to an "article." Many would say Wikipedia (http://en.wikipedia.org) betters paper because it allows for linking between the articles. Wikipedia allows anyone with access to the Internet to author or modify articles on the Wikipedia Web site. On most Web pages, following a link to a file that doesn't exist gives you an error. In contrast, following links to nonexistent documents in a wiki creates new documents that the user can add to and modify. This means it is easy to build an entire Web site using a wiki-based Web server. The Wikipedia uses this model and invites the world to participate. RSS is used in many wikis today, too. The newsfeed tracks changes to each document in the wiki.

The wiki is likely the best example of the intent of the original World Wide Web, envisioned by its developer, Tim Berners-Lee. Berners-Lee's original vision of the Web was in fact Read/Write, but the "write" capability didn't arrive immediately. When developers finally established the means to allow users to "write" in an otherwise static Web page, the Read/Write Web was born.

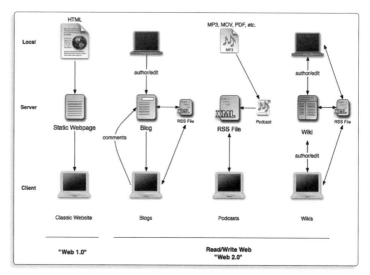

Figure 0.1 This diagram contrasts the key concepts behind each medium, from a classic version of the Web page to current iterations of blogs, podcasts, and wikis. The top "local" row represents what you, the author, may create at your end. The "client" row includes visitors to your Web site. In the case of blogs and wikis, the content is placed directly on the server through a Web page. This is why "Web 2.0" is commonly referred to as "the Read/Write Web."

THE READ/WRITE WEB IN EDUCATION

A Time for Change

In his book *The Singularity is Near,* Ray Kurzweil tells us:

> *Most education in the world today, including in the wealthier communities, is not much changed from the model offered by the monastic schools of fourteenth-century Europe. Schools remain highly centralized institutions built upon the scarce resources of buildings and teachers.* (Kurzweil, 2005, p. 336)

Kurzweil also notes that the quality of education among our institutions of learning varies greatly, divided along patterns of variance in wealth. His book forecasts the near and far future of education, from access to high-quality education through virtual learning environments to merging with non-biological intelligence. He adds:

> *We will ultimately move towards a decentralized educational system in which every person will have ready access to the highest-quality knowledge and instruction. We are now in the early stages of this transformation, but already the advent of the availability of vast knowledge on the Web, useful search engines, high-quality open Web courseware, and increasingly effective computer-assisted instruction are providing widespread and inexpensive access to education.* (p. 336)

Kurzweil and other authors point to the MIT OpenCourseWare initiative (http://ocw.mit.edu) that is paving the way to free, high-quality content for higher education. The very idea of sharing and learning at little cost is a big shift in the economics of education. The University of California at Berkeley, Stanford University, and Duke's Fuqua School of Business are now sharing course content in the form of podcasts through Apple's iTunes University program (www.apple.com/education/products/ipod/itunes_u.html). Already, the California Open Source Textbook Project (www.opensourcetext.org) is following the lead of MIT and other higher-education institutions by providing free textbooks in a digital format through a wiki-based Web site.

The ease by which intellectual property can be copied at no cost will dramatically change our future economy and the way we learn.

Preparing for future work, however, is the job of educators now. We live in an era where "most work requires mental effort rather than physical exertion. A century ago, 30 percent of the U.S. workforce was employed on farms, with another 30 percent in factories" (p. 302). Today, combined, this figure is less than 6 percent.

Kurzweil predicts that over the next couple of decades, "virtually all routine physical and mental work will be automated" (p. 340).

CONNECTING PEOPLE TOGETHER

Think of blogs, podcasts, and wikis as methods of publishing and accessing content online. Remember that all three methods are relatively easy to do and don't require special expertise or training. Behind the scenes, RSS is the mechanism that makes publishing and receiving this digital content convenient.

Consider for a moment the changes brought about by Johannes Gutenberg in 1450 with the invention of moveable type and the Gutenberg printing press. Suddenly the ideas of others had a huge potential audience. The press changed communication forever. Today, our Read/Write Web is effecting similar profound changes in the wealthier nations, albeit at a much faster pace than Gutenberg's press did in book publishing. The $100 Laptop project (http://laptop. org) is aimed at bringing this power to less-wealthy nations, as well. I myself have experienced the Web's globalization effect in my own life. For example, suddenly your humble author, a musician-turned-technologist living in Virginia, is exchanging ideas about a recent Bach compact disc with someone in Canada. A music enthusiast from London not only reads what I write but also makes a comment on my review through my blog. In the following week, I respond to the comment, and yet another person joins in with news of what the recording artist is likely to produce next. We may be strangers, but we share a passion for Bach's music and the Read/Write Web enables us to collaborate and share. Similarly, millions of people today continue to form virtual communities online through blogs and discussion boards.

As an educator, I was excited in 2000 when I saw all the new technologies unfolding before me. I imagined a number of ways that teachers could become empowered. The first promise of the Read/Write Web in education is connecting people together. The second promise is access to time- and location-independent resources. While video conferencing provides us an exciting way to take two or more disparate classrooms and bring each participant together, webcasts enable us to interact live with others through video, text-chat, and sound over the Web. If we record that content, we can make it available in a convenient format via podcasting. Time- and location-shifting quality content offers an incredible convenience for the educator and the student.

THE IMPORTANCE OF COMMUNICATION BETWEEN SCHOOL AND HOME

In Goochland County, Virginia, since late 2005, the public school system has required every teacher to maintain a blog. My position there as a supervisor of instructional technology and webmaster involved moving us in that direction. The goal of the teacher blogs centered around increasing communication between the schools and the home. Communication equates to parental involvement. "Parents' involvement in their children's education is widely considered to have substantial potential for benefiting their children's development and academic performance, for improving schools, and for empowering parents." (Weiss, et al., 1998). It is no wonder, then, that administrators endorsed an easy-to-use mechanism for increasing teacher-parent communication.

I knew we had made a positive difference in the lives of families when a third-grade classroom worked together on a video storytelling project. Students watched their final movie (with popcorn at the ready), and afterwards one student raised his hand to ask his teacher, "Can you put this video on your blog so my mom can see it?"

But not everyone sees our teacher-blogging initiative in a positive light. In an article titled "Thou Shalt Blog," Kevin Bushweller from *Teacher Magazine* had this to say: "I can understand a requirement that teachers use e-mail, given its ubiquity, but blogs? Taking a format that first gained popularity as a mode of personal expression and turning it into a district-dictated bulletin board seems antithetical to the Web's free spirit" (Bushweller, 2006). What Bushweller may have overlooked, however, was the healthy connection between a teacher's use of (and comfort with) a given technology and the respective teacher's willingness to then use that technology to its greatest benefit with his or her students. Our teachers are ultimately blogging for the benefit of their students, not just for their own love of writing. Integrating the use of the Read/Write Web into our teacher's daily lives carries the potential to connect parents to what takes place each day in the classroom. At the same time, it sets the stage for using these tools with students for learning.

Don Tapscott and Anthony D. Williams, authors of *Wikinomics,* define the Read/Write era within a new type of economy, one of mass collaboration. "The new art and science of wikinomics," they say, centers around four ideas: "openness, peering, sharing, and acting globally" (Tapscott & Williams, 2006, p. 20). The authors describe the new Web as such: "Think of a shared canvas where every splash of paint contributed by one user provides a richer tapestry for the next user to modify or build on … the new Web is principally about participating rather than about passively receiving information." (p. 37) "The Web is no longer about idly surfing and passively reading, listening, or watching. It's about peering: sharing, socializing, collaborating, and, most of all, creating within loosely connected communities … If anyone embodies this new collaborative culture," the authors submit, "it's the first generation of youngsters to be socialized in an age of digital technologies. These youngsters are on the cusp of becoming leaders, and our research shows that this generation is different" (pp. 45–46). Tapscott and Williams describe the generation of "youngsters" born between 1977 and 1996 as having grown up "bathed in bits" and spending time "searching, reading, scrutinizing, authenticating, collaborating, and organizing.… Youth today are active creators of media content and hungry for interaction" (p. 47).

Teachers communicating with families at home serve as a small step toward addressing the many and constant changes in student's lives. We can think of this effort as having a hand in creating a colorful tapestry and building an online community. Blogging teachers begin the process of stepping into a new era where so-called digital immigrants start to feel comfortable among the digital natives—no doubt, the assimilation takes time and patience for all of us.

READ/WRITE IN SCHOOL

What if a school's success hinged on its ability to prepare students for an evolving, global society that demanded openness, peering, sharing, and acting globally? The culture that created the Read/Write Web is the same culture that favors openness and sharing, and is best typified by the open-source software movement. Volunteer programmers that created the Linux operating system worked together, piece-by-piece—each volunteer with a different and varied experience, and each in a different location across the world. This culture would do well to find a home in today's schools, in order for our students to find success today and in the future.

The Read/Write Web ought to have a place in schools for a variety of reasons. For one, the Read/Write Web is where both business and society have turned to grow and learn. Whether our tool of choice is Google, Wikipedia (http://en.wikipedia.org), or Ask Metafilter (http://ask.metafilter.com), we have access to a staggering amount of information online. The Read/Write Web is also a place where people make a living. "About one million of the most active traders on eBay have quit their day jobs and now make their living selling new and used goods full-time" (Tapscott & Williams, 2006, p. 100). "Lifelong learning" is frequently in the mission statements of schools and districts the country-over. During their school years and beyond, students will engage in endless opportunities to learn on their own. Teaching students how to self-educate using the Read/Write Web is an important new skill.

Students also deserve the experience of developing information and media literacies. The Center for Media Literacy (www.medialit. org) offers teachers resources for developing students' media literacy, which now includes, among others, both traditional media (e.g., commercials on television) and the nontraditional Read/Write Web variety (bias in blog entries, YouTube videos, etc.). The American Association of School Librarians provides resources online for addressing information literacy (www.ala.org/ala/aasl/aaslissues/aaslinfolit/informationliteracy1.htm), and AT&T provides information on "21st Century Literacies" (www.kn.pacbell.com/wired/21stcent/), broken into four areas: information, visual, cultural, and media.

Another reason to embrace the Read/Write Web? "Young People Urgently Need New Skills to Succeed in the Global Economy," reads the title of a report from the *Partnership for 21st Century Skills* (www.21stcenturyskills.org/index.php?option=com_content&t ask=view&id=276&Itemid=64). The report cites 70% of human resource officials feel that high school graduates fall short in critical-thinking skills, and 81% of human resource officials believe high school graduates are deficient in written communications. The good news is that by applying the Read/Write Web into the curriculum, teachers can provide students with opportunities to improve critical thinking, as well as both written and verbal communication. Beyond that, students can creatively explore other forms of communication, including film, music, and visual art. A podcast, for instance, requires planning, storyboarding, and writing before the podcast is published.

The Partnership for 21st Century Skills also calls for using "21st Century Assessments." The Read/Write Web can make an excellent medium for assessing student learning beyond the now-popular standardized test. Student blogs can become student digital portfolios. Student video projects can reveal, among many things, the student's attainment of critical-thinking skills. Collaborative, student-centered projects promote interaction with students from faraway schools, testing a student's progress in working with peers.

MOVING FORWARD

The real value behind the Read/Write Web is seen in both the content and the styles that emerge when many minds come together. Different from simply creating static pages on a Web server, the Read/Write Web builds communities, fosters shared knowledge and experience, and begins to virtualize the human experience. Your humble author is no futurist per se, but I do believe that the landscape ahead will build strongly upon today's Read/Write foundation.

We are seeing the start of perhaps another progression of society and technology when we note the pollination of Read/Write culture in several new areas. One example of this progression can be seen in the culture centered around hacking, which is done by folks Tapscott and Williams call "prosumers," the producer/consumers. Constructive hacking (not to be confused with the destructive or malicious practice of "cracking") incorporates the desire to create, to tinker, to improve the world. Many netizens share their hacking ideas through blogs and discussion boards. Whether it be to replace the battery and install a copy of Linux on their iPod, or to create new robotic toys by purchasing Lego Mindstorm kits and changing the software that controls them, prosumers are now taking the once-static products around them and are reusing, rewriting, and repurposing them.

The second area I see as a progression of our Read/Write culture is exemplified by the online phenomenon known as Second Life (http://secondlife.com). "Second Life residents are far more than just 'users,'" say Tapscott and Williams. "They take on virtual identities, act out fictitious roles and activities, and even create virtual businesses that earn some 3,100 residents an average net profit of $20,000 a year" (Tapscott & Williams, 2006, p. 125). Second Life, the creation of Linden Lab, is a three-dimensional virtual world where, as of this writing, over 2 million residents interact. "It's created almost entirely by its customers—you could say the 'consumers' are also the producers, or the 'prosumers'" (p. 125).

Now with an analog "universe" for teens, Second Life requires real interaction to truly appreciate. Virtual residents can buy land, sell services and products, and design and build virtual objects. Second Life is also currently being explored as a learning tool in higher education. And real-world companies have begun to hold demonstrations in Second Life. Linden Lab encourages its Second Life residents to build businesses and homes in their virtual environment.

Once you fly around in Second Life (yes, humans can fly and use a teleport to get around in the virtual environment), you might come to understand how this revolutionary interface could some day progress to a virtual, yet equal-to-real-life experience, certainly if technology marches along at the pace predicted by author Ray Kurzweil.

The Read/Write Web today is the bedrock of the future. It promotes communication, fosters interaction, and is becoming an increasingly important entity in modern society. It provides us access to a previously unfathomable amount of information and offers profound opportunities to exercise creativity. Yet, looking ahead, it is but one milestone on a plot of time. Just as businesses today are finding the Read/Write Web to be a worthwhile and lucrative pursuit, I trust we educators will find the Read/Write Web more and more rewarding in our mission to empower students through learning.

BOOK ORGANIZATION

I begin with a rationale for emerging, Web-based technologies and why they should be allies in every educator's arsenal of solutions.

Next, I explore how you can use podcasts, Web syndication, weblogs, and wikis. We will examine these technologies first as a convenience. These technologies can dramatically change our productivity as educators. You will learn how to use these tools to improve communication—for both what comes in and what you care to deliver.

Then I will focus on the use of podcasts, Web syndication, weblogs, and wikis in the classroom environment. I have also inserted tutorials on the use of these technologies for both school-based (teacher, administrator) and classroom-based (student) users.

We finish with online links that offer you more information, followed by a glossary of terms. I'll cover many of the acronyms and buzzwords that often make technology sound so foreign, so when you encounter unfamiliar terminology, check the glossary.

PART 1

School Applications

CHAPTER 1

Weblogs (Blogs)

The definite number of existing blogs is impossible to pinpoint, though some blog-tracking sites have estimated it at more than 60 million. Other sources claim as many as 112 million. Over a thousand new blogs are created each day. It took about ten years for the popularity of blogging to grow to this level. Today, blogs are being created by people in all walks of life and for innumerable reasons. You can use blog search engines like Technorati (www.technorati.com) or Google Blog Search (http://blogsearch.google.com) to read blogs of interest on any topic imaginable. As I've mentioned, blogs are Web sites that are usually organized around short writings called "posts." Some compare them to journals or "logs." Many of these blogs have links to other Web sites and blogs of interest. Bloggers, or the folks who maintain these Web sites, often share personal and candid "from the hip" commentary about everything from their reflections on travel and work to the politics of the day. They typically enhance these public writings with video, photos, and an invitation for visitors to comment on what they have posted.

The rise of blogs as a medium for electronic publication has helped coin the term "Read/Write Web." Progressing from a Web of read-only content to one of read-and-write content has been no small transformation. For an analogy, we might compare it with music. Listening to music can set a mood, change the quality of a car ride, and make us smile. Yet, when (if ever) we try to create the same sound, how many of us can actually produce the same quality of music that comes from an accomplished ensemble? Blogs (an intrinsic ensemble) enable us to make some serious noise with our "air-guitar" keyboards. In the so-called blogosphere, we can now play alongside the band.

THE ANATOMY OF A BLOG

There are many ways to identify a blog. Many times authors will label the blog as a "blog," "weblog," or "online log" somewhere on the site's homepage. The content in blogs is not based on a document concept, but the concept of a news story, or "post." The front page of a blog typically displays any number of posts, arranged in reverse chronological order. Each post is likely preceded by a header, or post title.

Individual blog posts also include a hyperlink called a "permalink." Permalinks are a way to link directly to one individual blog entry, no matter where it appears on the page at the moment. Because blogs are updated frequently, the ability to find this information in the future could be difficult without permalinks. Many blogs include two versions of the post: the dynamic homepage version and the static version that others can point to from their blogs.

Linking to other blog posts on other Web sites is also common to blogging. You can include your favorite blogs in a "Favorites" list in a sidebar, called a "blogroll." Or you can extend the content or a "conversation" going on in another blog within your own blog, using a special kind of link called the "trackback." Trackback links appear in the other author's blog; they link readers from there to your own blog.

Blog posts also include metadata. Metadata is information about the blog post, including the date or time it was posted online, the content author, and, in some cases, the keywords that describe the content. Many blogs employ a category system where authors can "file" their writings.

Conversations can unfold in blogs, too, when authors host space for other people's comments or questions. If you are familiar with a Web-based guest book, a blog extends this idea further by generating a guestbook-style area for each and every blog post. Less personal than an e-mail message to the author, the blog comment is available for others to read. It is for this reason that we can compare the practice of blogging to reading and writing. Of course, history has presented these opportunities for read-and-write communication before—through, for example, pamphleteers, Talmudic scholars, and even a journal or diary writer. Blogs support our human need for communication and conversation on a grander scale.

THE EASE OF BLOGGING

Blogging is technically an easy feat, as long as you have something to communicate. Today, blogs can be updated in a variety of ways, from composing a few paragraphs to uploading camera-phone pictures. For teachers interested in publishing on the Web in my schools, blogs became the tool of choice because they were easy to use.

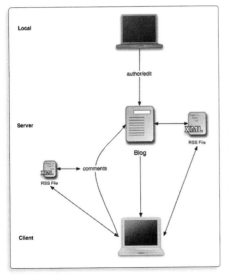

Figure 1.1 While we "blog" on our own computer, the content lives in a database on a Web server. Each blog typically has an associated RSS file for tracking blog posts, and some comment systems have a second RSS file for tracking the comments on a blog.

Before we blog, we need to acquire a blog. Here, two choices await us: host your own blog or have someone else host it for you. There are benefits and drawbacks to each choice, depending on your needs, desire for control, and your technical expertise. We cover many of these choices in chapter 7.

BLOGGING EDUCATORS

While many readers may have already decided "Yes, I would like my students to blog," they may not have considered if they, themselves, should maintain a blog. There are, I believe, many good reasons for teachers to have a Web-based presence. You can extend learning beyond the classroom walls by presenting learning opportunities online, and you'll find that a blog is a great tool for offering convenience to students and families. What many teachers find agreeable about blogs are the ease of publishing information, the informal, yet organized presentation of ideas, and how quickly they can link to other content found online. The blogs outlined in chapter 7 make this possible without an authoring application or a degree in HTML.

With so many families online today, it makes sense to harness the Web as both a communications and instructional tool. The methods we use to reach our students and their parents at home are varied: newsletters, e-mails to parents, school-mailed bulletins, and telephone messages. A teacher or principal's online blog is one more method we can now add to this list, and it is one that need not rely on student delivery. The interactive nature of some blogs, what with their comments and trackbacks, can invite conversations that both parents and students can find engaging. Once families are subscribed to your blog, each item posted is delivered to them, much like an e-mail message, with RSS syndication. This link of communication can be an effective way to keep parents informed and students on track.

GETTING STARTED

Some educators find blogging difficult at first. There are choices to be made before starting, such as "Where will I blog?" and "How much will it cost me?" Educators may also ask, "Is anyone out there reading my blog?"

In order to make the process go smoothly for our teachers in Goochland County, Virginia, we decided to host and maintain the blogs on our own school server. We could then best assist with many of the logistics involved in starting the endeavor, as well as maintain responsible control over the content that was to be published.

Our project started small, with ten teachers. The most important things I could do to help these teachers was to encourage them to keep posting (more frequent updates lead to more visits) and to visit other blogs. Blogging really is an activity unto itself, one that is best understood through praxis. By reading other people's blogs (each with their own topics, perspectives, and styles), the teachers were able to apply what they had learned to their own blogs. Typically, this included short, informal, and frequently posted thoughts and ideas that typically pointed to other writings and Web sites.

Several years later, I now offer tech support for every teacher and principal with a blog in our district. My superintendent requires each teacher to maintain a blog. I help support the endeavor by meeting with teachers and showing them how to do some engaging things with their blogs (like adding multimedia content they or their students create). Since the time we began blogging with just ten teachers, we have continued to supply the server space for all blogs and materials that teachers share online.

Our blogging blossomed for a number of reasons. First, our leadership valued what blogs could do to bolster communication between the schools and families in the community. Second, teachers received feedback on what they began to publish online: Parents were making it clear that they valued a "virtual look" inside their children's classrooms. Third, our students, many of them already Web savvy, were finding new ways to learn through their teachers' blogs.

Our principals value teacher blogs, too. Using a news aggregator on their own laptops, principals in my district track what teachers are publishing online using the RSS newsfeed associated with each teacher's blog. At a glance, they can see what is being taught, and they can see documented success when student work, pictures, and videos are shared online. One principal encourages his teachers to publish their lesson plans via blog as well.

My superintendent practices what he asks his teachers to do. His blog is popular with parents who want to know what is going on across the district. The superintendent's blog is used to answer questions from the public and to share news and announcements. While he was skeptical about maintaining a blog at first, he was soon encouraged by the positive feedback and blog comments from parents.

Whether or not educators blog as part of a district-wide initiative or through a free, online account by themselves, the educator's blog is a powerful communications tool. Once educators have alerted students and their families that the blog exists, they will likely find that it transforms the quality of both instruction and communication with students.

GETTING BLOG SAVVY

The best blogs by educators have something to say. They document best teaching practices. They share the successes teachers are having with students. They display student work. They continually reinforce expectations teachers have for their students. They spell out the course ahead for learning. They empower parents with information for continuing learning at home. In short, they become a trusted resource for the education of each student.

The best blogs, inside education or out, have less to do with design aesthetics and more to do with content. Granted, a well-designed site (theme, color, typography, usability, and layout) can indeed contribute to a positive public reception, but good blogs are good primarily due to the quality of the writing, the significance of the content, and the frequency of updates.

It is easy for me to tell when a teacher has made a leap forward with their blog. Creativity takes over, and the blog becomes an indispensable tool. "Show me how to put this on my blog," is always a welcomed question. Savvy bloggers in schools are those educators who depend on blogs as tools that can help them share the wealth of online content. And blogs can also help them organize their professional lives. Educators see great value in the Read/Write Web—in the potential for *everyone* to share online! Once educators see, feel, and experience this power to publish easily and quickly, they begin to share this enthusiasm and knowledge with their students.

In or out of the classroom—with blogs, podcasts, wikis, and the like—teachers can only benefit by understanding the tools themselves. The savvy blogger knows the power of publishing his or her own content. They get feedback from parents. They see their own students relying on their content when the students are online. Savvy bloggers know blogging and its reach because they have experienced it firsthand.

When computer technology was first introduced in many schools, its initial use was to boost productivity. Typing worksheets and administering tests became easier. Lately, this focus has rightly been adjusted to integrate the use of hardware and software to teach, learn, and improve the achievement of each learner. Savvy teacher/bloggers are not all experts, but they don't have to be—they own the valuable experience of practice, and they continue admirably forward knowing that blogging can make a significant difference for their students.

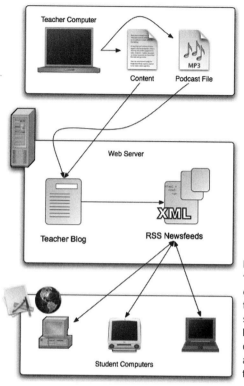

Figure 1.2 Educators can "push-out" content to students through blogging and the blog's newsfeed. When students subscribe to your blog via RSS, they automatically receive blog content and podcasts published through your blog.

WHAT SHALL I WRITE ABOUT?

Between the extremes of starting out and achieving blog-savvy Zen, this question is likely to appear in the educator's mind: "What shall I post today?" If we focus on the blog as both a communications and productivity tool, we might come up with some worthy inspiration.

Write about what makes you love your job. When bloggers write with enthusiasm and emotion, readers note the dynamic content. While blogs by educators should always be professional, showing your human side to both parents and students can help all readers relate to you and your position as an educator.

Write about your experiences as an educator. Some educator/bloggers (or educator/bloggers-in-training) are using the blog as a self-directed journal. Be careful here. I have read blogs by student-teachers and first-year teachers that share too much about their thoughts—both good and bad—about teaching. Always consider your audience and the amount of information that identifies your students. The reasoning behind this practice of self-journaling during student-teaching is to benefit the student-teacher and to enable a mentor or professor to monitor that student-teacher's progress as a teacher. In cases where you are asked to be completely honest, consider a password-protected blog, a nonpublic blog, or obscuring your identity and where you work.

What are students learning? What projects and activities do students find engaging? Ask students to report on the blog what is covered on a given day. Share the standards being covered with parents. Provide parents with questions to test their children's learning at home.

Post examples of student work. The publication of student work through the blog can be a motivating practice for students. Artwork is easily displayed with photographs, and written content is easily published with a "copy-paste" into the educator's blog. Remember that students own the copyright of their own work, and you must get student and parent permission before posting student work. A student's privacy must respected and strictly enforced.

Share your expectations. Expectations teachers establish at the start of a year can go a long way toward establishing good behavior, good work ethics, and improved student motivation. Teachers who share their expectations through the blog are continuing to communicate and reinforce behavior, school citizenship, and motivation.

Post questions that you would like students to answer. One teacher I work with posts bonus questions for students. Knowing that students read her blog at home, she can anticipate some of them coming to school the next day after having focused at home on a particular puzzle, riddle, or research question. She awards extra points and special privileges to students who answer the blog questions.

Extend lessons, offer independent practice, and encourage the reading of a blog. Every lesson taught does not always fit neatly into predetermined classroom time. Extend a lesson through the blog by offering a missed lesson's closure through a blog post. Teachers can use the blog to post homework assignments. Some teachers post homework only through a blog to encourage students to read the blog.

Start a conversation. As we will explore more when discussing student blogging, the real appeal of blogs is the reader's ability to participate by posting comments on what was written. Include content on your blog that invites student responses. Ask students to respond with silly content to lighten the mood, or use comments to perform informal assessments of the content being covered in class. Some blogs created by teachers are centered around various projects, and they invite students to participate by making regular comments to the blog, which can be easily monitored and approved before they appear online.

INTEGRATING WITH BLOGS

There is no question that blogs are but one phenomenon of a growing, progressive movement of technology innovation that schools are now beginning to explore. Blogs many times get a bad rap with schools because of social networking sites such as MySpace, which offers blogs and blog-like features that connect online participants, but sometimes contain negative content. The blog phenomenon offers us, however, a legitimate writing and communications tool to connect our own content to other content on the Web, easily and cheaply.

I lament that some schools are blocking access to blogs. There is no doubt that blogging is a powerful tool. And just like with the power tools we might use at home, effective, safe use takes care and a willingness to assess both benefits and dangers.

Blogs can have an incredible impact on education—indeed, they already have! Blogs can empower teachers and students alike. I believe that blogging teachers help set a standard for what responsible, appropriate blogging can look like. When the media tells us student bloggers have no great role models for what to communicate through the Read/Write Web, I look to our teachers to explore their potential in online, self-publication. When families, teachers, and students have reasonable access to the Web, a blog can be a great tool for communication and for making learning interactive, convenient, fun, and worthwhile.

CHAPTER 2

Wikis

Wikis are Web sites that can be quickly updated. The term was first used by Ward Cunningham between 1994 and 1995. Cunningham borrowed the term from the Hawaiian word *wiki,* which means "quick." His "WikiWikiWeb" became a tool for individuals to collaborate on documents by simply clicking an "edit" button on a Web page and changing the content—without knowing HTML or how to transfer documents between computers on a network.

While blogs are short posts organized on a Web page in reverse-chronological order, wikis follow more of a document-based model, where each page (however long), is part of a complete site. Since Cunningham's original WikiWikiWeb was developed, many other variants of a "quick Web" have developed. Likely, the most widely used and well-known is Wikipedia, the free online encyclopedia.

Wikis complement the Read/Write Web for many of the same reasons blogs do. Using wikis does not require technical knowledge, and content online can be authored completely within a Web browser without any additional dedicated applications or knowledge of coding. Like the software behind a blog, wiki software lives on the Web server and the content is stored in a database.

A wiki site can be a profoundly productive component in the work of any organization that has ready access to computers. Many open-source software projects today rely on wikis for contributors and users of free software to co-write the manual and documentation. There are benefits for using wikis in education as well. In this section, I will document how wikis can be used by teachers and administrators. In chapter 10, I will discuss wiki use in classrooms.

WIKI CHARACTERISTICS

Different wiki servers offer different capabilities and features, but most wikis are defined by several key characteristics. The overriding principal of each one is that content can be updated by anyone, quickly and easily.

Traditionally, wikis host documents on a Web server that can be not only read by anyone, they can be *edited* by anyone. This idea is alive and well on Wikipedia. There, you can search for an article on any topic, read it, and if you have something to add, you can click "Edit" and make changes.

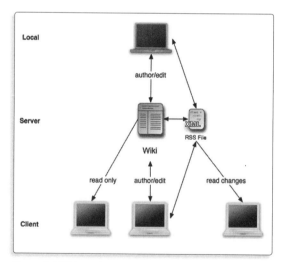

Figure 2.1 Wikis can be edited by you, but they can also be edited by others (clients). Some wikis limit the "powers" of editing to just reading for some users, and some wikis can keep documents password-protected altogether. Some wikis include an RSS feed for tracking changes to the wiki.

Wiki documents, or articles, are composed in some form of "wiki-text," a formatting syntax that controls the look of the text (boldface, italics, etc.) and provides links to other Web sites and wiki pages. Editing a wiki page is much simpler than using HTML, but it does include using some formatting symbols to structure text when displayed on the wiki pages.

Each time I introduce wikis to educators, they are engaged by the novelty of being able to manipulate a Web site so easily. I ask them to think of the wiki as a book. "It's a book we can all share in reading. But in addition, we can make corrections, add new pages, and make new links between the pages." Many wikis include the ability to utilize multimedia files such as graphics, audio, and video—going far beyond text editing.

The wiki system you choose may have a history feature, like Wiki-pedia. This ensures that bad edits to the documents contained within can be "rolled back" to an earlier version. Wikis can save every document version ever made. This is something that our word processors (typically) cannot do! If you are tracking users on your wiki system, each change in a wiki document will show when changes were made, and by whom. Most wiki systems also include a search function that spans across all documents created in that wiki.

PICK A WIKI

As with blogging, the hardest part about starting with a wiki is *where* or *how* to start. Three wiki engines I recommend that you can install and run on your own server include MediaWiki (the engine behind Wikipedia), PmWiki, and Instiki. Free and paid-for wiki space is available from many providers. One option popular with educators is Wikispaces by Tangient, LLC. In the fall of 2006, they gave away 100,000 free wiki spaces to educators. Another is PBwiki, who claim that a free wiki is "as easy to make as a peanut butter sandwich."

MediaWiki

MediaWiki (www.mediawiki.org/wiki/MediaWiki) is open-source and free for installation on your own server. Required, as of version 1.8, is Apache or Microsoft IIS (Internet Information [Web] Server), PHP 5, and MySQL 4, or PostgreSQL 8.1 database. The combination of Apache, MySQL, and PHP is popular for many Web-hosted, open-source software packages. Because it runs the popular Wikimedia Foundation's Wikipedia Web site, it has a large following and its interface is consistent if you have experience using Wikipedia.

Along the top of each MediaWiki document, called an "article," are tabs connecting the article to a "discussion" page and a "history" page. This separates the main content into a separate area that encourages discussion of the content and the article's history.

MediaWiki is a good solution if you have the technical knowledge to install it or have the assistance of a technical staff. Once installed and configured, it is relatively easy to use: just begin adding content. Media-Wiki sites can be configured to accept content changes from anyone, or from only registered users. It works well with high-traffic sites but choices for changing the appearance of this wiki are limited.

PmWiki

Another open-source wiki engine, PmWiki (Patrick Michaud Wiki, www.pmwiki.org) is a popular choice for installing a wiki on your own server. Like MediaWiki, PmWiki requires the presence of PHP and either Apache or Microsoft IIS on the server. PmWiki does not use a SQL-based database.

PmWiki uses "wiki groups" to organize its documents, or pages. Conveniently, each group can have different access credentials, such as unique passwords and access rights (read, write, and uploads). Because of this control, I have adopted use of this particular engine successfully to accommodate a number of groups in our school district. Each real-life group (e.g., leadership team, media specialists, technology team, etc.) gets their own wiki group and their own passwords. While everyone uses the same server and the same software engine, the content stays separate between groups.

PmWiki is easy to use and adopts a wikitext (formatting syntax) that can be controlled with application-style "buttons" to apply the codes. If a user forgets how to make text bold, the user can simply click the "bold" button while editing to assign boldface formatting. While MediaWiki offers a similar feature, I prefer how it works in PmWiki and feel the wikitext syntax is easier to learn.

Instiki

Instiki (www.instiki.org) is yet another wiki engine that will run on any platform, but it requires the Ruby scripting language. Its software includes the database, Web server, and related components. Because a "double-click" binary version exists, it is an attractive option for users with no knowledge of a command-line interface who want to begin to explore hosting their own wiki.

I have found Instiki works best when hosted on a teacher's own computer for use in the classroom. With the potential for easy setup, along with Instiki's portability, it is an attractive solution for hosting your own wiki server. On our network, both instructors and students use the Mac OS X operating system that supports "Bonjour" network addressing. In short, this gives each computer a unique name on the network that students can remember and bookmark. Going to the teacher's wiki page is as easy as finding a favorite search engine.

Instiki supports two popular text-formatting languages to edit pages in wikitext. These are called "Textile" and "Markdown." Instiki lacks the multimedia support of MediaWiki and PmWiki, and it lacks the ability to build accounts with passwords or wiki groups.

No matter which platform you operate from (Mac, Windows, UNIX, Linux), wikis are powerful editing tools for building documentation, establishing an electronic curriculum, organizing meetings, recording school board events, and collaborating on a variety of projects that require input from a variety of people. Wikis can live happily alongside other server software, so no new hardware is necessary for intranet or Internet Web servers to include wiki services.

CREATING A WIKI DOCUMENT

Most wikis allow users to create documents simply by linking to them. While linking to a document that does not exist will give you an error on most Web sites, in a wiki (when the linked document does not exist), it gets *created*. In this first example, I will create a table of contents by linking to not-yet-created pages.

The typical way to create a link in a wiki is to use double-brackets around the text you want to link. Another method for creating links in a wiki is to write a so-called camel case word. This is made up of

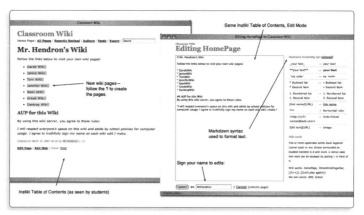

Figure 2.2 Instiki times two: Here I have set up a Table of Contents for students to begin adding content to the wiki on my computer. On the left, what they will see. On the right, what I created after clicking "edit." From their own wiki page, students can create as many wiki pages as they need.

two words together (without a space) and using capital letters to start each word. For example, *WikiWiki* is written in camel case, while *Wikiwiki* is not. By writing out new pages in camel case format, it is easy to create links on your site.

Wikispaces, the online wiki service mentioned above, uses Media Wiki-style wikitext. It also supports button-style visual editing, similar to a word processor. Each user in the system can create a number of spaces. The spaces created with their free service can be either open to the public to read and edit, or open to the public to read—with editing privileges assigned to members you approve. The service's subscription-based plans include wikis closed to the public. One feature unique to Wikispaces is the ability to add keyword "tags" to each wiki page. These can be used to search for content and the content of other creators within Wikispaces.

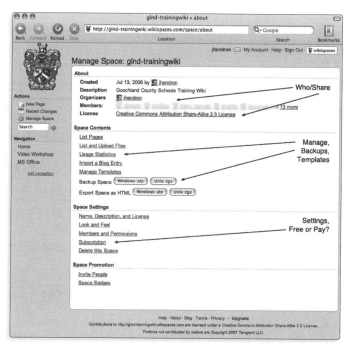

Figure 2.3 With the free version of Wikispaces, I invited Wikispace members to participate in a wiki for a staff development training session.

Adding External Files

Most wiki engines allow the uploading of external files, such as documents from word processing programs, PDFs, or images for display or download within wiki documents. In the example here, we will upload a graphic file to a PmWiki page.

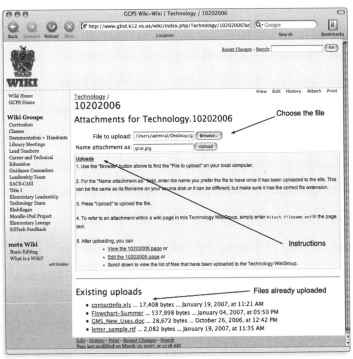

Figure 2.4 PmWiki offers support for the upload of files. After clicking an "attach" button, following a link offers this screen, where the file is chosen off your local disk. Uploaded files are shared among each wiki group.

USES FOR WIKIS BY EDUCATORS

My experience has shown that once a wiki is set up, it is a far easier endeavor for teachers to begin using than blogs. The concept of the "document" over a "blog post" has ties to a more traditional individual document model of information on a computer. The pages that make up a wiki resemble traditional word-processing documents and Web pages more than do the posts that make up a blog.

When establishing a wiki for use, teachers need to know the wikitext system in use for your wiki (the codes for manipulating text, making links, etc.), the policies for making changes to wiki pages, and how to sign in or sign pages within the wiki.

WHO WROTE THAT?

Many organizations use the wiki as an intranet—an internal Web site for use only within the organization. After establishing this model, I found making the wiki public on the Internet with password protection gave everyone better access to the content we placed online. In order to make the system work, however, we require everyone to "sign" each page when changes are made. While this happens automatically with MediaWiki when users log in, anonymous posts can be made with other systems. Using PmWiki, I use group passwords (everyone shares the same password), and pages cannot be updated until they are signed (after making a change, the user's name must be entered before the changes can be saved).

Requiring a sign-in does several things. It tells us who last made changes; but, more importantly, it enables us to track use of the wiki and all content by that particular author. This becomes paramount when tracking student contributions. When wiki collections become large, it is nice to be able to search for your own content using your name, to see the notes and contributions you made to the wiki's collection.

WIKI IDEAS

In my district, our first wiki project replaced an aging, customized database solution for enabling staff members to sign up for after-school technology classes. The home page of our wiki offered a bulleted list of staff development classes. Each class is linked to its own dedicated page, where teachers could sign up. To attend the class, teachers modify the page, which includes the class location and time, by adding their names to a list.

Our next wiki project involved transferring our PK–12 curriculum to a wiki engine. Already electronic, we took the output of a customized database and created new wiki pages for each class. The wiki's home page contained links to each grade and subject (K-Language Arts, 3-Science, etc.). While all teachers could access the curriculum online, we limited access to changing the curriculum content to our cadre of lead teachers.

After acclimating educators to a new "wiki culture," more wikis blossomed and were created for a variety of uses. Wikis come into

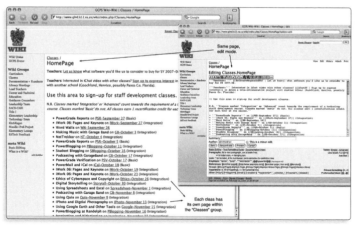

Figure 2.5 A wiki serves as a common space for teachers to sign up for after-school classes, and to check for updates for class locations and meeting times.

play whenever people need to share access to information quickly, and to share responsibility for creating and updating that content. Imagine teachers sharing study guides, lesson plans, and resource documents via a wiki. Teachers across halls, and across districts, can augment original documents. One wiki server can accommodate all of the uses in the following list, and more.

- ☐ Curriculum

- ☐ Lesson plans

- ☐ Sign-up sheets

- ☐ Daily announcements

- ☐ Daily attendance

- ☐ Virtual bulletin boards

- ☐ Meeting agendas, Minutes

- ☐ Staff development documentation

- ☐ Staff handbooks, Policy manuals

- ☐ Class notes, Handouts

Many meetings that take place with committees, leadership, and beyond in the school environment can be facilitated with a wiki. Before a meeting convenes, committee members can add content to the virtual agenda page within a wiki. Members can each maintain their own "notes page" on the wiki to take (and share) meeting notes. Notes never get lost, as they are maintained on the wiki.

Most recently, we have been using wikis to design staff development handouts, "cheat sheets," and instructional guides used in training sessions. Teachers can access the handout online or print a copy. When the guide requires updating, everyone now has access to the updated version. The built-in wiki history enables others to reference previous versions.

Many schools have manuals and guides that receive minor updates each year. With a wiki, these changes can be made online and immediately available. New copies no longer need printing, and everyone saves on paper use.

In conclusion, wikis can offer connected persons within your school or office a convenient and resource-saving solution for maintaining both written and multimedia content. The democratization of authorship with wikis means that everyone can take part in the knowledge-building by contributing their own content.

Some wiki engines offer support for syndication (RSS). If, for example, the superintendent has assigned a committee to research the feasibility of building a new school, he or she can monitor the progress made on the project via RSS updates (as the committee adds content to the wiki). Principals can monitor new lesson plans submitted by teachers via RSS. In the same way, teachers can monitor new lesson plans submitted by colleagues in their subject areas.

PRODUCTIVITY WITH THE READ/WRITE WEB

The use of wikis in education can increase productivity when everyone has access to networked computers. Wikis allow everyone equal access to content. Wikis also allow the ability to create and modify content within a framework that preserves changes, document history, and enables one to search via text, keyword, or the author's name.

The use of major wikis such as Wikipedia is often a debated topic in the education world. No one can ignore that content in Wikipedia is plentiful, ever-growing, and international. Users conducting searches on major search engines such as Google choose Wikipedia-sponsored matches, thus authorizing the content and sending Wikipedia at the top of search-engine hits. The democratization of online choice has identified Wikipedia's content as an authoritative source.

Many educators are split on their opinions of Wikipedia. Since Wikipedia's wikis are being visited and reviewed by thousands of visitors each minute, the content is in a constant state of flux. Articles are corrected, augmented, and, in some cases, just as current as the content seen on CNN Interactive or Yahoo! News. Many today, including author and professor David Weinberger, believe there is a new, emerging face of online content. Wiki content is certainly current and new, but its accuracy is sometimes up for debate.

While the accuracy of every article on Wikipedia is not pristine, might we alter our concept of an encyclopedia? A comparison of scientific articles between Wikipedia and the *Encyclopaedia Britannica* appeared in *Nature* (Giles, 2005) and showed the accuracy of the two sources at roughly equal levels. (Among 42 science entries tested, the average science entry in Wikipedia contained approximately four inaccuracies; Britannica, approximately three.) Wikipedia, then, and the sites that will follow its lead, may offer us both greater breadth and depth than traditional sources.

Wikis, like the Web, are always "under construction." Our experience using wikis as educators has shown us that the contribution of many versus one is sometimes messy, but it is often more enlightening and valuable. Preparing students for a world that offers so much information so easily—albeit in a sometimes-messy state—is a great reason to use wikis in the classroom. We will explore this further in part 3, Classroom Applications.

CHAPTER 3

Podcasts

In addition to the Read/Write Web, perhaps with the growing popularity of podcasting we should begin calling the Web the "Listen/ Broadcast Web." Podcasting is a process of publishing/broadcasting on the Web that uses Really Simple Syndication (RSS) to deliver multi-media content to end-users. Its popularity is due in large part to the popularity of portable MP3 players, the growing access to high-speed Internet connections, and the increase in free and engaging content.

Podcasting has a lot of potential in education. It was embraced first in higher education, when professors began sharing collections of content such as audio files of class lectures. Universities today are sharing significant amounts of content, both as a convenience to their paying students and as a public relations tool. Several schools have partnered with Apple to create a podcasting presence through Apple's iTunesU service. Universities are using Apple's servers to host content, and the students are using iTunes software to download and access this university-published content.

The K–12 arena is slowly catching up, as teachers are exploring pod-casting for use in the classroom and in projects where students are becoming content creators. Some schools are also using teacher- and administrator-created podcasts to increase communication, extend classroom walls, and simply appeal to a growing number of students who carry MP3 players and cell phones that can playback podcasted content.

HOW PODCASTING IS UNIQUE

Like many new things associated with the Read/Write Web, podcasting, too, was born out of a desire to make life online easier. The audio and video content that users are creating today has a history that precedes podcasting, which began in the fall of 2004.

Podcasts are simply a new way to distribute this content. With podcasts, the focus shifted from individual files of content to the source or the content author. Compare this with how popular video Web sites work, such as YouTube. On YouTube, users conduct searches, and relevant videos appear on the screen. In many cases, we do not care who produced the videos, we simply watch them. If we like the video, we can comment on it, rate it, or even link to it from our own Web site. Podcasts, on the other hand, are Internet-based broadcasts that we commit to watching or listening to, because the podcast medium is built upon subscription.

The number of podcasts available today, many times an example of "prosumer content," is staggering. Two days after release of the program, Apple reported one million podcast subscriptions (Wickipedia, n.d.). With podcasting as a delivery method, and today's high-quality editing and recording equipment in the hands of so many computer enthusiasts, traditional pathways to publication and broadcast are no longer necessary. In fact, many of the Web's most popular independent podcasters have little or no previous broadcasting experience.

For a hypothetical analogy to a podcast subscription, let's say you're in a grocery store and you notice a new magazine for sale in the check-out aisle. "Hmm ... this looks good," you say to yourself, as you drop the magazine into your shopping basket. You pay now for this single copy, and after reading the magazine later and deciding the articles were valuable to you, you send in that little card inside, thereby beginning your subscription to the magazine. Each month thereafter, the issues come, for as long as you care to pay, receive, and read the journal.

Podcasts work in a similar way, except that the subscriptions typically do not cost money (for now, the vast majority of podcast-created content is free). And instead of noticing this content in your grocery store's checkout aisle, perhaps you first discover podcasts through an online directory, such as Yahoo! Podcasts (http://podcasts.yahoo. com) or the iTunes podcast directory (www.apple.com/itunes/store/ podcasts.html). There, you can preview podcasts online and download individual episodes. The magic, however, takes place when you subscribe.

SUBSCRIBING TO PODCASTS

One appealing trait of podcasting is the ability to take this content "on the go," using an iPod or other portable audio or video device. A particular class of application on the computer manages those podcasts you subscribe to and can organize those media files and keep a portable device up to date with the latest podcast episodes. This application is called an "aggregator," but it goes by many other names, including "podcatcher" and "newsreader." Each time a content publisher creates and publishes a new podcast, they advertise its availability by updating the RSS file associated with the podcast. It contains a list of all the available episodes.

To subscribe to a podcast, we connect an aggregator with an RSS file. It, in turn, does the rest. The aggregator regularly checks with the servers that the RSS files point to and effectively asks "What's new?" A comparison of the RSS files will tell your aggregator if new content is available. If it is, then the aggregator downloads the new content.

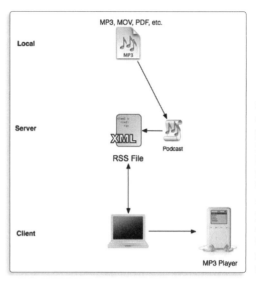

Figure 3.1 As someone subscribing to podcasts, you are the "client." Both you and the publisher (see "Local") exchange files from the same Web server. Podcast directories do not hold podcasts; instead, they simply connect you with the servers that podcasters have used to publish their content.

Finding podcasts is no longer difficult, now that many good directories offer easy access to RSS links. Once you find an RSS link, feed it to your favorite aggregator and subscribe. Just like a search engine, however, every directory presents podcast links in different ways, and all the collections are not equal. Because these directories are just that—links to content that others have created—you will find that some podcasts have "dried up" and no longer provide fresh content.

SEARCHING, SUBSCRIBING, AND LISTENING WITH iTUNES

One of the easiest ways to find and download podcasts is with Apple's free iTunes software. While required for synchronizing an iPod to a computer, it can also be used with the iPod for ripping CDs, listening to Internet radio, and burning favorite mixes to CD. Since version 4.9, however, iTunes evolved to include an RSS aggregator function. It also links to a popular podcast directory, which makes finding and subscribing to podcasts a snap.

Figure 3.2 iTunes organizes popular podcasts in various categories and allows users to search for podcasts in the same way it directs users to their favorite music with their iTunes Store.

The amount of content in the iTunes directory may seem staggering. Some podcasts are highlighted, some are listed by popularity, and more await us behind buttons in various categories such as comedy, television, or business. To find podcasts dealing with the world of education, click on the "Education" category in one of the iTunes boxes. "New and Notable" education podcasts appear at the top, while featured podcasts dominate the page, and "Top Podcasts" flank the right-hand side of the iTunes window. Many categories appear the same way, enabling users of iTunes to explore. Always popular in the Education category are foreign-language podcasts, with their promise to help us learn one of the world's many languages. The best in this category combine audio with visuals.

Navigating through more featured podcasts reveals 5 pages with approximately 21 podcasts per page, with podcasts about everything from test preparation and world languages to technology use in schools and high-school-produced podcasts. But are there only some 125 educational podcasts? No—the iTunes directory for podcasts is large, but the point-and-click interface only reveals so much. The built-in search function in iTunes that you use to search their store is also tied to finding podcasts. If you know something about the title or the author of a podcast, this search capability can be used to find it.

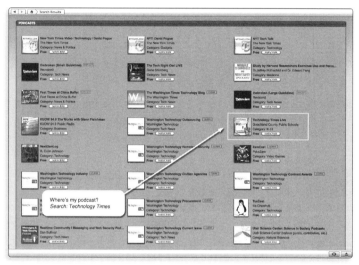

Figure 3.3 Using the search function within iTunes returns results from both the music store and the podcast directory. And with Mac OS X's parental controls, you can restrict students from listening to podcasts marked "Explicit."

Once you find a podcast of interest through iTunes, you can double-click an episode's title to preview the podcast. Clicking on a "Subscribe" button will do just that—it will join the RSS file associated with the podcast (that you found through the iTunes directory) with iTunes' ability to use that RSS file, and then "ask" for new episodes when you are online. Podcasts then get organized in a section of your iTunes library. The first time you subscribe, iTunes downloads the latest episode and then configures itself to download future episodes (until you stop listening, at which point it suspends your subscriptions). It also lists older episodes from the RSS newsfeed file and lets you download those one by one. If you do use Apple's iPod, this

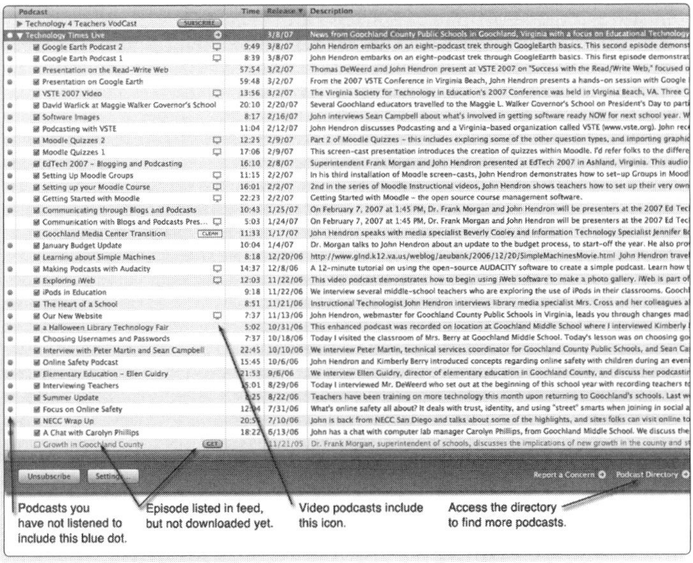

Podcasts you have not listened to include this blue dot.

Episode listed in feed, but not downloaded yet.

Video podcasts include this icon.

Access the directory to find more podcasts.

Figure 3.4 Pictured here are episodes already downloaded after subscribing to *Technology Times Live!* Use the disclosure triangle next to each podcast feed to show/hide the episodes from each podcast. In this picture, *Technology Times* is visible; *Technology 4 Teachers VodCast* is not.

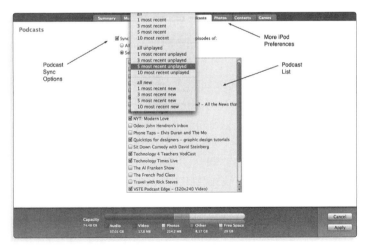

Figure 3.5 On my copy of iTunes at home, I have tried many different podcasts. Fortunately, iTunes allows control of which podcasts I want to sync with my iPod. I can even control which episodes from my favorite podcasts I want to include for on-the-go listening. Tabs along the top (which appeared in version 7 of iTunes) control the preferences for my iPod, when it's connected to my computer.

method of using iTunes to download and organize your podcast files is the easiest for transferring them to an iPod or iPhone.

Yahoo! Podcasts, Podcast.net

Two popular Web-based services, Yahoo! Podcasts (http://podcasts.yahoo.com) and Podcast.net (www.podcast.net) enable you to discover, listen, and subscribe to new podcasts, all within the comfort of your Web browser. They offer a Web-based version of the iTunes experience.

Both services enable visitors to listen to podcasts through the Web page, but they also both work with third-party applications such as iTunes. These are but two of many services attracting visitors who need help in locating podcasts. The process of finding, subscribing, and listening to podcasts has improved greatly since podcasting first emerged. When you create your own podcast, you gain better exposure when reporting your newsfeed URL to multiple directories.

MANUALLY SUBSCRIBING TO PODCASTS

In the example procedure below, I'm going to subscribe to a blog that is being used to publish podcasts. We will find and copy the RSS newsfeed link from the blog and then return to iTunes. We will use iTunes to subscribe to the podcast "manually." This same process can be used to subscribe to podcast feeds with aggregators that support attachments.

1. First, visit a blog that is being used to publish podcasts. We need to find a badge, or link, that points to the RSS newsfeed.

2. On some systems, subscribing can be as easy as clicking on the link. Let's say four links are available—

two show possibilities for "RSS 2.0" and "RSS Podcast." But which is the one we want?

3. "RSS Podcast" points to a link with the header "itpc://." This protocol activates iTunes (i.e., if iTunes is installed, clicking this link will automatically subscribe to the podcast using iTunes).

4. "RSS 2.0" points to the same file, but it uses the protocol "feed://"—used by Apple in Mac OS X. Because we're using iTunes, either link will work. If we want to use this in an online aggregator, we can replace "feed://" or "itpc://" with "http://".

5. Right-click on the link to "Copy the Link."

6. In iTunes, go to the Advanced menu—"Subscribe to Podcast." Paste the link you copied and click "OK." iTunes will then attempt to subscribe to the podcast.

COMMUNICATION

A 2003 report on school improvement from Mid-continent Research for Education and Learning (McREL, 2003, p.3) states that, "In a well-functioning education system, it is understood that parents and other stakeholders need to be apprised of progress being made, obstacles that have been identified, and solutions being implemented." The report also says that "an effective communications program builds understanding and support, solicits input, and strengthens the long-term success of reform efforts." The report also suggests a key element to a successful communications program "fosters dialogue whenever possible."

Many educators already realize the importance of communication between the school and the home. As children grow into adolescence, parental involvement declines. We all know that parental involvement in the school's mission of education can be a factor in a student's success. Research has shown that the higher expectations parents have for their students, the better students do. A 2004 Harvard Family Research Project report (Patrikakou, 2004) said, "Robust teacher preparation for the schools of the 21st century should reflect the multitude of research findings pointing to the importance that parent involvement has in all stages of the educational process."

School administrators and teachers can use the Read/Write Web to increase communication and maintain high expectations in both directions. Continued communication between the school and home can foster positive feelings between teachers and parents. Podcasting is but one medium available today to educators in reaching parents and the community.

A podcasting principal? Why not? A teacher-podcast published each week to review the week's events? Definitely. Not only does the "educator as podcaster" scenario work for providing one-way communication into the home, it also puts a powerful tool in the educator's hands for using podcasting with students.

Are there disadvantages of using podcasts as a communications medium? Currently, audio and video files are not easily searchable. Text is far easier to search and find when end-users (parents and community members) are using conventional search avenues to find your content. Podcast files (audio and especially video) also tend to be large. Homes with no Internet or slow-speed (modem-based) Internet access likely will not have the opportunity to see or hear your communication. In addition, there are many families to whom podcasting is so new, they are not confident in using aggregators and portable devices to see, hear, or watch podcasted content.

Conversely, because podcasts are a subscription-based media, getting parents to subscribe is the major battle. Once they have, you know you have a reliable mechanism for getting communication to the home. In many communities where a digital divide is being addressed through one-to-one initiatives (through, for example, community-wide wireless access and through initiatives aimed to supply low-income families with computers), podcasts are an attractive communications medium for educators.

MAKING PODCASTS

Apple has published an online seminar (free with registration) called "The Podcast Recipe: Producing a successful show," at http://seminars.apple.com/seminarsonline/podcast/apple/index.html?s=203. This three-part video webcast includes input from voice talent Joe Cipriano, independent podcaster and home recording enthusiast Paul Garay, and Apple's manager of iTunes directory, Pete Alcorn. The online seminar is 25% marketing for Apple's solutions in the production and enjoyment of podcasting, but the seminar also offers a lot of insight into producing a quality podcasted production and serves as a worthy introduction.

Planning

Before we create a podcast, it is important to think not only about the episode, but also about the "show." Since podcasts are modeled after radio and television shows authored by one person or an entity, the planning requires looking at the small details (all the elements within each episode) as well as the larger picture (what holds each episode together to form a cohesive whole; for example, a connecting theme, as well as a musical motif or other familiar sounds heard throughout the series). The big picture can simply be a regular schedule of classroom news reports, a regular stream of staff development tutorials, or even broadcasts of school board meetings.

Will each episode be a puzzle piece that, together, forms a whole, or will the structure be simpler? When creating podcasts that are instructional in nature, the big picture becomes a matter of instructional design, and it will likely dictate how each episode consistently unfolds.

What media is best suited to your content? Video? Audio? A stream of pictures? While many podcasts are aural, a growing number of enhanced podcasts incorporate chapters and still images that use a Macintosh tool called GarageBand. Enhanced podcasts for Windows Media files are more difficult to produce, although Jake Luddington offers a solution using Microsoft's free WindowsMedia encoder (www.jakeludington.com/project_studio/20051004_windows _media_enhanced_podcast.html).

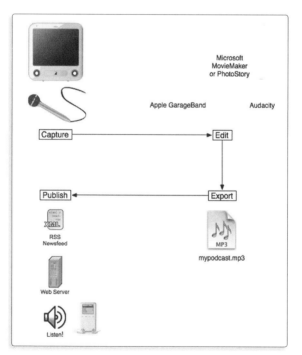

Figure 3.6 A podcast production cycle includes four steps: capture, edit, export, and publish.

Your Audience

Who is your audience and what is their attention span? What do they already know and what do they want to learn or experience?

In any type of presentation, we must first consider the essential elements that good communication demands. The best podcasts address their audience and get to the point quickly. They are also presented in universal formats. Using obscure codecs to encode your digital creation will only require the audience to install the additional requisite software.

MP3 format is preferred for audio podcasts. It does not require platform-specific software and can be played back using just about any computer or portable media player. Video Web sites such as YouTube use Flash-based video (FLV). While these videos playback well on many computers, the most popular portable video players (e.g., iPod, Zune, or Sony PSP) work well with MPEG-4-encoded video. MPEG-4 (sometimes called "AAC" for the "Advanced Audio Coding" found at the core of MPEG-4), like MP3, is not platform-specific.

In short, know your audience and then address them with brevity and functionality. Economize your podcasts in terms of length, and make enjoying and transporting the content you produce easy for your audience.

THE SUPERINTENDENT'S PODCAST

In the example that follows, we will be producing an audio podcast that our superintendent of schools plans on producing eight times throughout the school year. Here are some assumptions we are going to make about his audience.

☐ 90% of students in the school district have at least one computer at home with Internet access.

- ☐ 75% of students with computers at home have broadband access.

- ☐ 40% of the parents and guardians with computers at home regularly read one blog or more.

- ☐ 78% of families with computers at home own only Windows-based PCs; 14% own Apple Macintoshes; another 8% have both operating systems.

- ☐ 48% of households own an iPod.

- ☐ 60% of households own an iPod or another brand of portable music player.

- ☐ 12% of parents surveyed have listened to a podcast, or are familiar with what a podcast is.

- ☐ 85% of parents surveyed say they have seen or met the superintendent of schools before.

Some of these details might have an impact on what choices we would make in planning this podcast. Since so many families have Internet access, it is decided that producing podcasts will be a worthwhile communications initiative. A fair number of households are familiar with the concept of a blog and read blogs, but fewer are familiar with podcasts. Including information on how to subscribe and access podcasts will be important in making the initiative successful. A mixture of platforms at home would suggest staying central with an open format for the podcast, such as MPEG-4 for video, or MP3 for audio. Roughly half of households, however, own iPods which means they have QuickTime installed. QuickTime is required for iTunes on both Macs and PCs, and it opens the way for creating enhanced podcasts using GarageBand.

The superintendent decides that his podcast series will focus on "safe schools" and "holding high expectations." Since a theme to the series exists, we will establish a short musical introduction that communicates the series' ideas of safe schools and high expectations. The superintendent has decided that since 85% of parents are likely to recognize him, audio will be sufficient for the podcasts. An alumnus from the district's high school composed an uplifting fanfare that the school band plays each year at their year-end concert. A 10-second clip of last year's band has been recorded in WAV format and will be used to introduce each episode in the podcast series.

Whether your decisions for planning a podcast are this well-informed or not, it is always wise to have good reasons for each decision you make in the process. For example, if there is something that your audience has in common (like a familiar subject-related fanfare), this presents an excellent reason to work it into your podcast's theme or musical motif. If you are not so fortunate to have uplifting fanfare music (as described in our example district), some editing packages include royalty-free jingles and music clips. The online service Freeplay Music (www.freeplaymusic.com) sells licenses to use their collection in podcasts and audio blogs.

Superintendent's Podcast: *Introduction*

To identify the start of each podcast with the same cue, lending cohesion to the series, we will use the following lines: "Where safe schools are a priority; where high expectations are held each day: Welcome to Superintendent Jones' Podcast from Smithfield Schools!" Perhaps we could have members of the superintendent's advisory committee record that introduction. We will follow it with the high school band's fanfare music. As we plan the first podcast, it will be important to maintain a similar format or formula for the podcast's sections. While content ultimately drives the format of how a podcast is put together, the consistency between episodes offers a professional touch that listeners will appreciate.

Our podcast introduction will be used at the head of each podcast. After it is put together, it can be exported as a separate file and introduced into each new podcast production. Whenever you save clips to re-use, make sure you do so in a high-quality, uncompressed format (typically WAV or AIFF). Re-compressing the file over and over (if it is saved as MP3 or another compressed format) will degrade the sound quality considerably. Consider what happens when you photocopy another photocopy; the same thing happens to sound.

Details for using Audacity, the editor used here in our example, can be found in chapter 5.

Superintendent's Podcast: *First Episode*

In order to make the process easy, we are going to supply our superintendent with a voice recorder. He has agreed with us to keep his podcasts short: 5–10 minutes. The flexibility offered by a digital voice recorder means he can record an episode whenever it is convenient, and he can use the portable device to interview teachers, students, or parents in the schools.

For each podcast, we will begin a new project in Audacity. Voice recorders from different manufacturers record audio in both compressed and uncompressed formats. Let us assume in this case our superintendent's voice recorder produces CD-quality WAV files (16 bit, 44.1 kHz). Use the Project menu > Import Audio command to load each WAV-file clip into the Audacity project. In Audacity's timeline, use the time-shift tool to align the clips in sequence.

Superintendent's Podcast: *Export*

In order to export the Audacity project as MP3, LAME is required. LAME (which, curiously, stands for "Lame Ain't an MP3 Encoder") is an open-source MP3 encoder. While it has to be installed separately, instructions for doing so are included on the Audacity Web site (http://audacity.sourceforge.net/help/faq?s=install&i=lame-mp3). Choose File > Export as MP3. In the next dialog box, you can supply tags for your MP3 file. This is a good opportunity to name your podcast episode and identify the author.

Superintendent's Podcast: *Publish*

Publishing our podcast requires first transferring the MP3 file to our Web server. Transfers can be done via FTP (file transfer protocol) or from the desktop via a mounted network drive. The second step for publication is the generation of the RSS feed to enable subscriptions. For this example, we will use an application to generate the newsfeed.

FeedForAll (www.feedforall.com) for Windows and Macintosh, and Feeder (http://reinventedsoftware.com/feeder/) for Macintosh are two popular desktop applications that make easy work out of creating the XML file for RSS 2.0, instead of having to hand-code the RSS. This is how they work:

1. Upload your media file to the server via FTP.

2. Note the address (URL) of this file.

3. Create a new entry in the RSS-creation application.

4. Include metadata for the podcast, including a description about the content you have recorded.

5. Save your work, and you will have an updated XML file.

6. Transfer this file via FTP to the Web server.

7. Point the public to this file with one of many RSS badges or buttons from your Web site.

By publishing a link to the MP3 file, we are helping get the message out to folks who do not own iPods and who know nothing about podcasts, but who want to hear an audio file we have created.

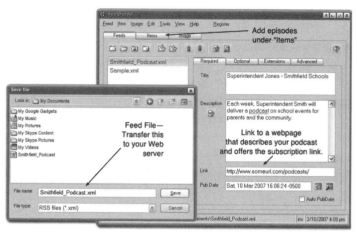

Figure 3.7 The first step in creating an RSS feed is to name the feed and podcast, then save a local copy to your documents. Pictured: *FeedForAll.*

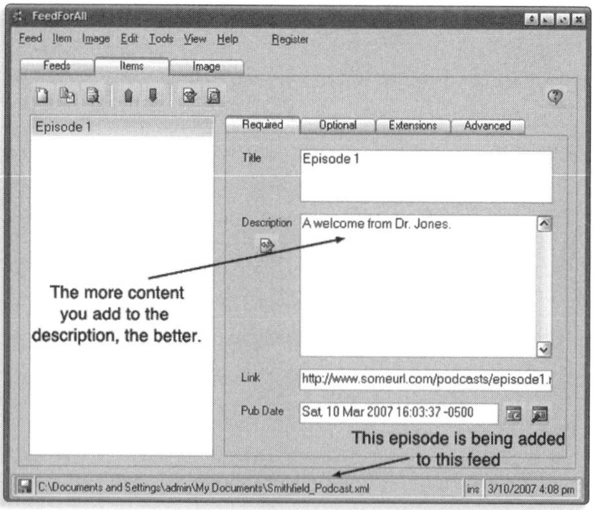

Figure 3.8 Under the "Items" tab, we describe our first episode. Descriptions should include a summary of the podcast, which can help to alert listeners of the content contained within. Include terms that might be used as "tags" or keywords to help identify this episode in a search.

By publishing a link to an RSS newsfeed, we are publishing a podcast with the promise of future episodes to come. Used alone, these are adequate publication means, but together, we can reach a wider audience.

MORE ON PUBLICATION

Generating your own RSS with a specialized application is not the only way to publish podcasts and to create RSS. We can also use a content management system (CMS) that utilizes RSS to publish our podcast. This method uses server-side software to do the magic. This method can also aid us in not only creating the RSS, but also by publishing standalone links to reach podcasting neophytes.

What is a content management system? A CMS is server-based software that enables us to quickly and easily publish content online without having to provide code. It typically dumps content into a template that can be professionally designed. The CMS often uses a database for the Web site's back end to organize content contributed by one or thousands of content creators.

Today, one of the most popular classes of CMS is blogging software. In chapter 7, we detail publishing a podcast through the free Blogger system with help from another free tool called FeedBurner.

THE BEST PRACTICES BLOG

One of my principal responsibilities in my current position is staff development. I'm the guy who figures out how something works and then shows fellow educators how it can be used in their classroom. But when you bring together teachers from different grade levels and disciplines, things tend to get too generalized. I have found that focused development offered to a limited population of teachers (say, 3rd- and 4th-grade math teachers) on dedicated staff-development days is effective, and teachers appreciate being led by fellow educators. Since our district is small, we use many of our own teachers to promote their best practices in the classroom—both with and without the use of technology.

In this example, teachers contribute to a group or community blog that supports the publication of podcasts—both in PDF (Portable Document Format) and audio (MP3, AAC) formats. The theme? Best practices. The artifacts they upload to the blog as podcasts are collected together with narrative testimonies and then published on a district Web server. The blog becomes a resource for other education professionals for improving the quality of instruction within the school district. Principals, lead teachers, and department chairpersons may be assigned to choose superlative lessons that are included in this blog.

While many blogs earn "community status" by offering readers the option of posting comments, I use the term here to denote blogs that have multiple authors. Many content management systems support blogging, and many support multiple roles for community blogs. Your community blog can identify a) one administrator who can post and edit all entries by all contributors; b) content creators that can create posts and then edit and delete their own posts; and c) editors who cannot post themselves, but can edit the content created by others.

One example of a community blog is the "Coach's Corner" hosted on our Web server (www.glnd.k12.va.us/weblog/coaches/). Different athletic coaches, including the athletic director from our high school, use this blog to post details about the various athletic events taking place. Metafilter (www.metafilter.com) is yet another, well-established example of a community, multi-author blog. Multiple authors not only contribute content to be published, but also chat amongst themselves and generate content in response to what has been published. Many technology-forward companies, too, are now hosting blogs for the development of projects and practices.

Getting Best Practices Online

The reports teachers publish in the blog can be comprised of three pieces. The first is an audio file that documents (in their own words and voice) why their pedagogical practice makes a difference. Secondly, within the blog text, they will include a short description of their best practice, including keywords that will help identify the practice in a search. The third component is optional, but an additional entry or podcast may include a PDF file of a worksheet, rubric, or supporting document to help illustrate the best practice. Remember: Podcasts can be any single multimedia file, including a PDF. Since RSS can only embed one multimedia file per "news item" or blog entry, teachers will not be able to publish both the audio file and the PDF in one blog entry as a podcast. The PDF file can, however, be added as a link, if supporting documentation for the best practice is required.

The blog can serve as a valuable resource for teachers within the district. Publishing this content in podcast format will deliver the content to other teachers who welcome the challenges of new, innovative, or revolutionary pedagogy. One of the Web's most powerful features is its ability to connect people and provide them with a virtual space for the sharing of ideas and content. When teachers contribute to a best-practices blog and podcast, they not only make a contribution to their profession, but also add to their skills for communicating via blog and podcast. This can only increase their confidence in introducing these new and emerging tools to students. (NETS•T: I.A., I.B., V.A., V.B., V.C., V.D.)

WRAP-UP

Podcasting offers content creators on the Internet a new method for getting their music, video, and other multimedia out to an audience through a novel subscription method powered by Really Simple Syndication (RSS). Multimedia files such as MP3 audio or MPEG-4 video are enclosed within the RSS newsfeed file. Educators can use this technology to increase the variety and frequency of communication that goes home to families. Increased communication between parents and teachers is often identified as a sure way to better the achievement of students, especially as they mature.

In this chapter we created hypothetical podcasts in open formats (MP3) using free and inexpensive software (Audacity, FeedForAll). Using either a standalone RSS-creation application or popular blogging software, publishing a new episode to a podcast is just a few clicks away. The blogging method of publishing podcasts offers several benefits. Content creators (in our example, the superintendent) can also be content publishers, since using blogging software is easier than generating RSS feeds and transferring files via FTP. If the blog used to publish the podcast is enabled with a comment feature, then a second benefit opens up: two-way communication for both parents and community stakeholders who wish to respond to blogs with their own comments.

Podcasting is still young and is now being examined by researchers inside and outside the world of education. While audio and video blogging preceded podcasting, the unique aspect of how podcasts are published and received—through a subscription model, using software that can automatically grab new content—is likely what has made podcasting's popularity soar.

Once your first couple of episodes are published and announced on your Web site, it is time to consider publicity. You can publicize your podcast (to make it easier to find) by submitting the RSS feed you establish to various podcast directories. Two recommended directories include Apple's iTunes directory (www.apple.com/itunes/store/podcaststechspecs.html), and Podcast.net's directory (www.podcast.net/addpodcast).

CHAPTER 4

VoIP and Synchronous Communication

It was not long ago that a high school principal told me he was talking to his students about their cell phones. "Guys," he said to them all, "you're allowed to bring them here to school, but you can't use them without permission." These students wondered if this rule also applied to "texting" (sending and receiving text messages). Curious about how students were communicating, he asked them more about texting. He soon realized that many of his students prefer this means of communication. "How much do you use e-mail?" he asked them, and then learned that "e-mail is for formal things." The students explained to him that e-mail was analogous to the formal hand-written letter, and texting was like an informal note or phone call. "It seems already e-mail is old-fashioned to our kids," he told me. The attraction to texting has much to do with its instantaneous nature. Texted messages are typically short and use abbreviated forms of words. What is especially appealing is that text messages can be sent without great disruption or interference—if you can't read the message right away, it will be waiting for you later.

Another story comes from a school-based computer technician whose son attended the same school. The student had been working on a project for two weeks, putting together a PowerPoint presentation for his science class. Students were told to bring in a floppy disk with the presentation, and when this particular student showed up with a USB flash drive instead, the teacher was suspicious of the new technology and would not let him put it into her computer.

"My son was angry," his mother, the technician, said. "He just wanted to show his presentation—he and his buddies had worked so long on it!" The boy secretly texted his mom about the incident, telling her about the inability to use the flash drive in the teacher's laptop. She dispatched a technician to the room, who calmly changed the teacher's mind, and the group was able, finally, to show their work that was saved on the flash drive.

The right-now appeal of instant messaging by telephone or computer has carried over to synchronous voice communications. Known as "VoIP" (Voice over Internet Protocol), services such as Skype and Gizmo Project enable online users to communicate by text chat, voice, and video over high-speed Internet connections. Skype and Gizmo Project start by mimicking other instant message applications, including AOL Instant Messenger (AIM), Yahoo! Messenger, and MSN messengers (e.g., Instant Messenger or IM). VoIP services expand on these free services by layering the ability to make and receive phone calls. These same technologies that let the public make inexpensive phone calls can be used in schools to connect learners to resources beyond their traditional classroom walls, with voice- and video-based communication. When learners on either end are connected via two computers, this communication is free.

I have included using synchronous communications solutions in this section because I feel that in today's climate—where many schools ban or limit student access to cell phones, e-mail, and instant messaging—the use of synchronous solutions are best managed by the teacher. In my experience using Apple's iChat A/V software (a robust program for text, voice, and video communication that also uses Apple's brand of iSight digital video camera), we have enjoyed many successful exchanges between students in different school buildings. Among the most successful was the pairing of kindergarten students in one school with high school students in another. In this exchange, the high school students were being evaluated in their ability to read a book and teach a lesson as part of their participation in an early-childhood education class. The kindergarten students responded enthusiastically and enjoyed the opportunity to "interface" with their older peers. In each case where iChat software was used, it was active on the teacher's laptop computer and connected to an external LCD projector and speakers. Using software such as Gizmo Project, Skype, or iChat can be an inexpensive way to provide audio- and video-based conferencing to classrooms with access to high-speed Internet connections.

Gizmo Project

Currently, Gizmo (www.gizmoproject.com) offers free voice connections between computers and free calling from a computer to a phone. Gizmo works on the open-source Jabber network system, which means Gizmo users can communicate with those who have Jabber-based Google Talk accounts. Gizmo is available for Windows, Macintosh, and Linux, which makes it a great choice without worrying about another user's platform. To talk to other users via computer, you need a high-speed Internet connection, a microphone, and speakers or headphones.

Gizmo offers many features, including the ability to play sound effects during a call, the ability to record conversations to a digital audio file on your computer, and the ability to pinpoint the locations of the call on a map. One innovative use of Gizmo Project is for interviewing other folks over the computer or by phone. It lets you record the conversation. The WAV file that Gizmo Project produces can be edited and turned into a podcast. The obvious advantage to this is cost savings—if the interview is taking place online, the interviewer and interviewee could be separated by hundreds of miles, and yet there is no cost. Unlike the GarageBand solution from Apple, the Gizmo Project software works on all major platforms and can integrate an interviewee (by phone) into your recording.

Skype

Skype (www.skype.com), like Gizmo, allows users to make free phone calls from the computer. It adds the ability to correspond through a live video chat. Another feature unique to Skype is "Skypecasts," hosted calls where many online users from disparate locations can join together in group discussions. The user who creates the Skypecast moderates the discussion. Like Gizmo Project, Skype is available for Windows, Macintosh, and Linux.

Gizmo, Skype, and other services are positioned in strong competition and their features and costs may vary. Currently, however, Gizmo provides a free solution for voice communication and the ability to record these conversations. Skype likewise offers the ability to communicate via voice and video for free, and it offers the "party line" service Skypecasts, which allows up to 100 users to connect via voice online. Both solutions work cross-platform. While these services have been available first in Apple's iChat, both Gizmo and Skype were born out of the desire to marry traditional telephone connectivity with the computer.

iChat A/V

Every computer with Mac OS X includes iChat (www.apple.com/macosx/features/ichat/), a program that, like others mentioned previously, marries text and voice communications. iChat also includes video and supports users on the America Online network (AIM) and Jabber network. The third generation of iChat includes support for up to ten voice conversations at once, and supports up to four users with high-speed Internet connections in a video chat.

iChat does not include a record function within the program, but Apple does offer support for recording within GarageBand for podcast interviews. With iChat, first you establish a voice chat, then you switch to GarageBand to record the interview. Unlike Gizmo Project and Skype, iChat is not cross-platform. Instead, it uses open protocols (AIM, Jabber) to facilitate conversations with Windows users of AOL Instant Messenger and Jabber services such as Google Talk.

SYNCHRONOUS COMMUNICATION TOOLS

In the online world there exists a number of means for publishing content. Some of these follow a broadcast model, others introduce interactivity. Podcasting is all about subscribing to time-delayed content, but while podcasting is arguably the more interesting of all the emerging methods for online content publication, other methods (including wikis and variations on blogging) offer us still more possibilities for using text, audio, and multimedia to publish within an instructional setting on the Web. Among these are synchronous voice-based communications, audio blogs, standard text-based blogs, and multimedia-enhanced e-mails.

Social constructivist concepts of learning are supported by the Read/ Write Web, where individuals can express themselves and learn from knowledge generated in a social space. The tools in this chapter support the publication of content through audio blogs, video blogs, and podcasts. Synchronous communication, however, is different. Instead of its content being recorded, stored, and published, synchronous communication is live. Communal constructivism calls for learners to impact the content being learned. In student-centered classrooms, the opportunities for more diverse social interactions increase the opportunities for learning.

Let us now look at two applications of VoIP-based/synchronous tools: conducting an audio interview and a video conference.

Conduct an Interview

You give yourself authority when you invite the comments and expertise of others to your podcast. Participation by others can help establish the podcaster as a legitimate source of information who shares his or her expertise and enthusiasm on the topics explored. It also adds interest and variety to the content presented.

Some interviewees are more interesting than others. I have found some folks in our schools communicate naturally during an interview. Others require coaching and second-takes. You can maximize your time when working with interviewees by preparing them for the recording and taking the time to run through a test recording. You can use the computer to edit and amplify a weak speaker, but the less time you have to spend editing content, the more often you will be able to publish.

Potential problems for folks you interview include nervousness, projection, and what I call a "likelihood of rambling." You have to be quick-witted and sometimes commanding to stop an interviewee from taking over your time (and thus allowing you fewer questions to ask before the interview is over). Since podcasts are rarely timed in the way a real broadcast is, you do face the peril of gathering too much, in chunks that are too long to edit. On the other hand, you may not feel pressured to release a consistently timed podcast for each episode.

I prepare interviewees with the questions I am going to ask before recording. Sometimes this is through an e-mail a day in advance, and other times I have simply placed the questions on a table in front of us during a face-to-face recording. It can depend on *how* you conduct the interview. More often than not, I use an inexpensive USB microphone connected to my laptop for recording sessions. A USB microphone can cost between $20 and $50 and has one distinct advantage: the audio signal (from the microphone to your computer) is already digitized. As long as your USB bus is not being used to transfer other types of data at the same time (e.g., via an external hard drive or scanner), the only real limiting factor in the sound quality is in the quality of the microphone itself, not the signal path between the microphone and your computer.

VoIP-based recordings (made with Gizmo, iChat A/V, or with Skype combined with other software) can be scratchy and garbled at their worst, to at best a quality matching that of an inexpensive USB microphone. If I had the choice of using a VoIP product over a face-to-face recording, I would choose the face-to-face option. Yet, in my job as an educator, I do not have the time, patience, or means to travel and find guests for podcast interviews. But I can interview colleagues in other school districts during a 20- to 30-minute break. I can also arrange an interview for my students easily enough with classes in another school, or with community members who have broadband access to their computer.

For those interested in professional-quality sound, you obviously can throw a lot more money into your recording setup. Professional microphones can be used for podcasting, including those with XLR connectors. Analog microphones are plugged into a mixing board that amplifies the signal before it is passed into your computer, typically via a FireWire (IEEE 1394) connection or by high-speed USB. These better-to-best quality solutions can cost anywhere from in the low hundreds to several thousands of dollars. A number of portable recorders (made by companies such as EDIROL/Roland and M-Audio) record high-quality audio to removable cards (e.g., SD or CompactFlash) and can accommodate the same high-quality microphones.

When using high-quality source audio, podcasters can also take advantage of more robust editing applications. Among this class are Soundtrack Pro on the Macintosh and Adobe Audition for Windows. These applications offer fine-tuned editing capabilities, including the ability to eliminate noise from the recording and synchronize audio recordings with video. Professional tools and equipment are likely to be used by the public-relations arm of large districts, and in high schools focusing on media/television programs where students have the opportunity to use professional-level equipment and software.

The Gizmo Interview

This example can be adapted in many ways for a variety of classroom lessons. Instead of presenting this example in the context of a bona-fide lesson, I have focused here (as I have with the example that follows) on the teacher's perspective and how the technology at hand is used to facilitate an interview project. I have included a template, which should help both the person conducting the interview and the person(s) being interviewed. Depending on the current market, calls made with a VoIP solution such as Gizmo Project may incur a small charge when connecting to the interviewee's phone, or they might be completely free of charges.

Scenario: Students will use a podcast as a medium to develop questions in order to pinpoint what makes various citizens unique. They will articulate answers given by adults in spoken and written language.

Materials: interview worksheet, high-speed Internet connection, a Gizmo Project account with calling credit, Gizmo Project software, microphone

Possible pre-interview questions for students:

1. What is this person's name?

2. Where do they live?

3. When were they born?

4. Why is this person unique and well known?

5. Why do you think someone would value this person's opinion?

6. What interesting facts did you learn about this person?

Students use the answers to these questions to construct a paragraph introducing the interviewee. This can be read as part of the podcasting script. This portion of the interview can be recorded after the interview is conducted using the Gizmo Project software.

Next, students need to construct a number of possible questions for the interviewee. These should be sent to the person being interviewed before the interview takes place. Students can practice writing the letter, if preferred, and details about the interview time can be communicated through this letter to the interviewee.

Possible student questions for the interviewee:

1. What do you like best about your job?

2. What was your favorite part of going to school?

3. What heroes or role models did you have when you were growing up?

4. What do you see yourself doing in 10 years?

5. What advice do you have for students today?

6. What is the most interesting place you have ever been, and why?

Educators I have spoken to agree that shorter podcasts are better than long ones. Students should know that not all questions need to be asked. Part of the recording process can be a matter of fitting the interview into a predetermined time frame. Different students can also be selected to each ask a different question of your "famous person."

Better interviews often include the interviewer's commentary on the interviewee's answers. This is a more difficult skill for students. Students can be prepared for this with instructions to either agree or disagree with what the interviewee says, based on their own experiences.

To make the podcasting experience easier for younger children, some educators encourage the students to read their part in the script together, in unison. This method includes everyone, and no one student is singled-out in the recording.

Let's Interview Someone Famous

Your Name: _____ Date: _____

Who are you going to interview: _____

What do you know about this person already (three things):

What would you like to know when you meet this person (three things):

Before we create questions to ask our guest for the interview, consider the types of information that listeners to our podcast might be interested in. *Where are they from? Where do they live? Do many people know this person? Do they have advice for others? Where have they traveled?*

1. You will next write six questions on the back of this sheet in the first column.

2. Next, find out the famous person's name in Gizmo: _____.

3. Conduct your interview using Gizmo Project. Do not forget to begin, and stop recording before you deliver your questions!

4. Finally, write out the answers to your question in the second column on the back of this page.

Teacher Comments:

Figure 4.1
This is an example of a script that students can use to conduct an interview. Podcast scripts/templates should include both standard content that is repeated for each episode and areas for students to fill in that reflects their planning, research, and creativity.

Gizmo Project and Skype inexpensively bridge the world between having a traditional phone conversation and Internet-based telephony. A number of universities and organizations are already using Gizmo to build VoIP infrastructures for cost savings and convenience.

Gizmo Project's two pay services are "Call Out" and "Call In." Call Out lets you call phone numbers through the Gizmo Project client interface, and the rates are currently competitive with long distance phone services. Call In lets you obtain a phone number (currently) in the United States or Great Britain, regardless of where you live. When folks dial your number, you receive the calls on your computer. For U.S. residents, Gizmo Project offers over 30 cities where Call In numbers can be designated. Gizmo Call (www.gizmocall. com), their latest endeavor, enables users to make phone calls directly through a browser, using Flash.

Gizmo Project, like most instant-messaging applications, can easily expose children to strangers and content which might not be considered age-appropriate. Products such as Gizmo, then, should be used with children only under close adult supervision. Among Gizmo's features to watch out for is the "Party Line."

After downloading and installing Gizmo for the first time, you will have the option to sign up and create an account. Accounts are free. As with signing up with other instant-messaging services, the username you choose may or may not be available. While Gizmo offers an option to "remember" your credentials on each launch, I do not recommend using this in a classroom environment.

The main Gizmo Project window has four primary tabs: Home, Phonebook, Calls, and Conference. The Home tab displays your name and icon (avatar), status of your account (alerts, missed calls), and statistics if you are utilizing the Call Out or Call In services.

Your Phonebook in Gizmo is your list of online contacts, or "buddy list." You can either call these individuals or use text-based messaging to communicate.

The Calls tab shows you what calls have been received, placed from, or missed on your computer. Each record can be independently deleted or used to re-establish a connection with the previously called party.

The Conference tab provides instructions for establishing a conference call using Gizmo. Once you learn the identity of another Gizmo Project user, making calls is simple.

Use the "Member Search" feature to search for a friend by name. Add more friends to your Phonebook by using the large "plus" button to manually enter the Gizmo account names. Either way, adding contacts to your Phonebook is easy.

A status indicator within the Phonebook shows whether or not a particular user is online. For fun, I dialed one friend who was not online. What does this do? First, I hear an operator's voice that tells me this user is offline. The operator quickly, however, allows me to record a voice message. I talk into my computer microphone and leave a voice mail. Voice mail messages are forwarded to the other user's e-mail account as a WAV file. My friend received my voice mail message addressed from me, with the sound file included as an attachment.

Through Gizmo's preferences, you can also alert yourself of missed calls through SMS (Short Message Service) to a pager or cell phone. The latest version also allows call-forwarding, which uses Call Out minutes.

Let us try making a call with someone we might consider our "famous person" from our previous lesson's interview. If our famous person were a Gizmo user, the process would be as simple as:

1. Adding their username into your Phonebook.

2. Checking their online status.

3. If connected, double-clicking their username.

4. If not connected, dialing their phone number.

5. Starting the communication!

Calls made with Gizmo can be recorded as WAV files, which are stored on the local caller's desktop. If the caller(s) on the other end wish(es) to make a recording, too, they must also click to record the conversation. Gizmo alerts the other party that the call is being recorded. We would start our interview after the voice recording announced the conversation was being recorded.

Let us assume our famous person does not yet use Gizmo. We can still contact our interviewee by calling them on the telephone. This makes use of Gizmo Project's Call Out service. At the time of this writing, Gizmo Project awards each new account with a 25-minute free credit for calls within the U.S.

Gizmo includes a dial pad that enables us to dial phone numbers. Found on the dial pad are "blasts," which are sound effects you can "sound off" while the call is in session. These can be used to add interest to your interview; but when overused, they can distract and annoy the listener.

After you have dialed your phone number (including a "1" plus the area code for U.S.-based calls), you will hear a familiar phone ring from your headphones or computer speakers. I prefer using headphones when I use VoIP services on my computer. Doing so reduces the likelihood of feedback from speakers into your computer microphone.

Once you have established communication with the party on the other end, you can press the record button to start your interview. The last steps in this scenario are to conclude the interview, save the WAV file, and then open the file from your favorite editing application (e.g., Audacity, GarageBand, Audition, or Soundtrack Pro). After editing, you will compress the audio from one of these applications to create your podcast.

The Video Conference

A lot of solutions have been developed to connect users not only with audio but also with video. Among them, Microsoft Net-Meeting (Windows XP), Windows Meeting Space (Vista), iChat A/V for Macintosh, and now Skype with video are popular solutions. The iChat experience is limited to Macintosh users, and the Meeting Space experience is limited to Windows users, but Skype breaks the divide with a solution that includes Gizmo's telephony features and offers video "chat."

To connect two classrooms, both need Skype installed on one computer, high-speed Internet connections, a Web video camera, and video projectors with speakers attached to each computer.

Using the Skype service requires an account. To initiate a call with the other party (in this case, with another teacher's classroom), type their Skype name at the top of the Skype window, or add them as a new contact or "buddy." The main window in Skype will list your phone and chat-based contacts.

Skype's preferences have settings for video that must be first set for *enabling* video. Once you establish a "call" with another Skype user, you can click a video icon to turn the video functionality on and off.

Once a successful connection is made, the use of an LCD projector with speakers can bridge two classrooms together.

Synchronous communication is very different from the published Web we have been describing as part of the Read/Write Web experience, with wikis, blogs, and podcasts. There is no RSS involved with video calls. Yet at the same time, video chats can encourage a great deal of collaboration and excitement at seeing peers across the hall or the state, and make for an easy-to-use tele-collaborative climate.

Video Conference Ideas

So what might we do if we could connect two classrooms? And what might happen if we could take a laptop with a video camera into an area of interest (e.g., a park, museum, historical location, etc.) where high-speed Internet connectivity is available? Here are some ideas:

- An Expert Art Lesson: A recognized professional artist provides students with a lesson in a particular technique; students can then apply that knowledge at their school.

- Can You Hear Me?: Communicating and teaching American Sign Language (ASL).

- How Green are You?: Two classrooms connect to compare families' recycling habits and water usage in different areas of the country.

- How'd You Do That?: Teachers sharing best practices and technology solutions.

- Let's Learn Together: Language learners converse with students from another culture.

- Let Me Play for You: Musical performances by students are critiqued by a professional composer or musician.

- ☐ Let's Share Perspectives: A classroom debate.

- ☐ Let's Travel!: A staff member or parent travels to an area of interest and answers questions from the students who can see the traveler's new environment.

- ☐ Reading is Fun!: Second-grade readers with a Kindergarten or PK audience.

- ☐ Share Your Art: Students show their art projects to those in other classrooms and talk about the ideas behind their work.

From personal experience, I cannot tell you how excited students get over connecting with another classroom. "What might those kids look like?" "Will they be able to understand us?" "We better prepare and be ready for them!" The anticipation alone carries its own excitement.

Having an audience and the interaction of peers is, by itself, a great motivational factor in the learning environment that is provided by this new class of easy-to-use video conferencing tools.

Success with ideas such as these also requires planning and collaboration between instructors. Because each meeting across the network will be unique—and the learning objectives specific to what two or more educators will want to accomplish—I'll provide here ten guidelines toward making the most of your tele-collaborative experience using video "chat" software.

1. Establish a time to connect, and be flexible. One of the hardest challenges is finding that mutual time that both sides of the wire can meet together. Make the most of your time by being ready at the established connection time. Do not use your first class meeting as a "test" to see if things work. Instead, establish an instructor-only test first, before the two classes are to meet.

2. Check the other school/instructor's credentials. I have not heard of misrepresentation yet, but for good measure, make sure the other classroom you partner with is a real, authentic classroom. It may be in your interest to start by partnering with a classroom in your own school or district.

3. Share your plans. Sharing your lesson plans with the other instructor is important for both sides in meeting your goals for the collaboration. Include a section on how your students will be assessed, or whether you will flip-flop the responsibility of assessment by evaluating the other classroom's students.

4. Practice first. Practice using the video camera, speaking clearly and being careful not to shake the camera (a tripod always helps here). As well, practice using the computer and the software that will connect your students to the other classroom.

5. Speakers or headphones? Headphones work great when two people are communicating, because they can help minimize feedback (when the microphone "hears" the speakers and the sound becomes ever louder and distorted). But when an entire classroom is being broadcast, use speakers so everyone can be heard, but point them away from the microphone.

6. Optimize your time. Since meeting with another class can place a premium on time, consider breaking down your classrooms into smaller groups. For each meeting, have different groups connect, instead of the complete classroom.

7. Combine the experience with off-line collaboration. Many great video-collaboration efforts have started or

ended off-camera. Students can collaborate in other ways, too, including exchanging e-mails and media files (sound, pictures, movies) and sharing documents through Google Apps (see chapter 12, Newsfeeds in the Classroom).

8. Organize classroom control. Plan with the other instructor how the time on camera will be organized. Sometimes this is facilitated by devoting half of the conference to each classroom's presentation, while the other classroom simply watches. Because of the time delay between communication, keeping everyone's attention can sometimes be facilitated by putting one instructor "in control" for a segment (or for all) of the video conference.

9. Solicit student input. Ask for your students' opinions and ideas about what will make the video collaboration a success. Follow up the experience with student reflections.

10. Record the conference. Skype does not currently offer a solution for recording the video conference. Screen capture software such as Camtasia Studio (Windows— www.techsmith.com) and iShowU (Macintosh— http://shinywhitebox.com/home/home.html) can be used to capture your conference's audio and video for future reference, archiving, and sharing through your school's Web site, blog, or podcast.

VIDEO CONFERENCE PLANNING DOCUMENT

I have put together a video conference worksheet for planning a video experience between two classrooms. It addresses many of the guidelines listed above and can be used by both instructors from each classroom.

Each instructor has a space to outline what learning objectives pertain to the collaborative lesson. These objectives can be different for each group. The "Conference Sequence of Events" allows each teacher to plan out how he or she envisions the conference to take place. This may be reserved for each instructor's portion of the lesson, or it may outline the entire collaborative experience. If one instructor is put

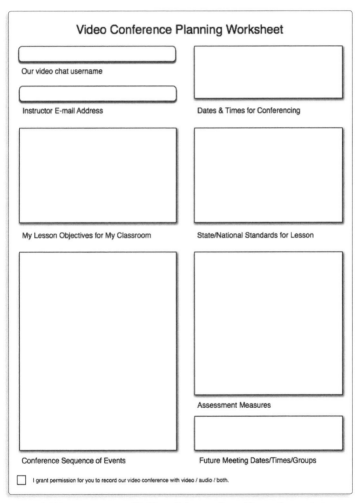

Figure 4.2 You may use or modify this worksheet to plan a video conference between two classrooms.

in charge of the lesson, the other instructor may elect to keep this area blank. In "Dates & Times for Conferencing," indicate the dates and times you plan on meeting. Be sure to include the time zone if you are conferencing with classrooms in other parts of the country or world, so everyone understands, for example, that your 1 p.m. means their 3 p.m.

The standards area is useful if your worksheet is shared with other educators, as they can quickly see if this lesson will meet their needs. The "Assessment Measures" are how you plan on assessing the objectives you have established for this conferencing lesson. These can include feedback from the other classrooms' students or instructor. I also included a "future" meeting time area for following up on an initial lesson. This area can be used to designate group meeting times, in the event smaller student groups are established for the video conference.

Both instructors should have copies of their own worksheet and their collaborator's worksheet before beginning the first video conference. To avoid shuffling more paper in our increasingly electronic world, this sheet (or a variation of) can be converted to a PDF- or Word-based document that can be e-mailed and shared electronically. If you are using Google Docs, you might also come up with a spreadsheet-based form for sharing instead.

Video conferencing has gained legitimacy in the world of education as a viable medium for facilitating distance education. And as technology advances, the ability to connect classroom spaces via nontraditional communication is continuing to get easier and cheaper. Now, with Skype (in addition to previously mentioned software tools from Microsoft and Apple), video conferencing can take place between any two computers. The use of a projector, speakers, and a good-quality Web camera can bring the experience to the K–12 classroom. To find Web sites that offer even more social spaces and lesson ideas for educators (to use video conferencing and VoIP tools in the classroom), see appendix A, Web Resources.

PART 2

Core Software Applications

CHAPTER 5

Basic Editing with Audacity

Audacity (http://audacity.sourceforge.net) is a gem for podcast-ready educators and their students for a number of reasons. For one, the software is open-source. This means it is free to use and is available on Linux, UNIX, Windows, and Macintosh platforms. If you learn the application on one platform, you can use it on another. Files in Audacity's native format can also be used between the different versions for each platform.

Despite being free, Audacity is rich with features. An entire examination of Audacity and all that you can do with sound editing would prove too comprehensive for this book. Instead, we will examine here some basic techniques for using Audacity to edit and prepare content for audioblogs and podcasts.

DIGITAL AUDIO

Audacity works with a number of file formats. Digital audio files use a number of different codecs, which are algorithms for how to compress and decompress the audio. Compression is a technique for reducing file size. Alongside each of these codecs are different settings to alter the efficiency of compression. For files on the Web, our goal is a small file that can be quickly downloaded.

On a compact disc, an hour of music is roughly 650 megabytes. That works out to around 10.8 megabytes per minute. The most popular compression codec for audio is MPEG-1, Layer 3. It is commonly referred to as "MP3." It returns, on average, a 10:1 savings in file size, so a one-minute MP3 file is around 1 megabyte. While Audacity enables us to slice and dice all kinds of digital audio files (including WAVE and MP3), it cannot create MP3 files. You may notice on the Audacity Web site a mention of LAME (Lame Ain't an MP3 Encoder). Follow the directions for your platform from the Audacity Web site for installing LAME. Once installed, you can use it as a plugin to export Audacity projects into MP3.

While MP3 is the most popular open format for compressed digital audio, there are others. The popularity of iTunes and enhanced podcasts has been echoed by the popularity of AAC (Advanced Audio Codec), which is based on the MPEG-4 standard. AAC files offer better compression savings than MP3, and they can support embedded graphics and metadata for the creation of enhanced podcasts. Currently, Apple's GarageBand is a leading tool in the creation of audio podcasts that include chapters, Web links, and digital pictures.

When your final Audacity project is complete, and you choose to save or export the file as MP3, there are many decisions to be made. MP3 files include "tags," which identify the file and are accessible to software—including the software on portable players—and get displayed as the song or podcast plays back. Providing tags that identify who is podcasting, the podcast title, and the episode, is a good idea. This metadata stays with the file, even when the regular filename gets changed. You will have the opportunity to apply tags to your MP3 file when you export from Audacity.

Another thing you choose when exporting an Audacity file is bitrate, or how much compression gets applied to the file. High bitrates make for larger MP3 files with better quality. With MP3s, we need to find a happy medium between file size and sound quality.

Does your podcast only use one stereo channel? If so, it is monaural (mono); this cuts the file size in half. I recommend using a bitrate of 64 kilobits. If your podcast project is recorded in stereo, or it uses stereo sound stingers or music, use a bitrate of 80 kilobits or 96 kilobits. You can compare these different settings by exporting a polished project a number of times—see if you can hear the improvement by raising the bitrates. The maximum bitrate for MP3 is 320 kilobits/second.

Some devices you use to record audio, including iPods with a microphone or a digital voice recorder, may create full, CD-quality recordings. These can appear as 16-bit, 44.1kHz WAV files or AIFF files. These CD-quality originals take up a lot of hard drive space on a computer. Using them for your podcast projects is good, because you do not need to sacrifice quality when you apply cuts, edits, and effects. However, once a podcast project is complete and you have exported a compressed version in MP3 format, you will likely want to erase these originals from your computer so they don't take up space. For archival purposes, you can back up original source recordings to inexpensive CD-R discs.

Now that we have discussed some of the issues you will encounter when finishing an Audacity project, let us jump in and begin a project.

AUDACITY EDITING WINDOW

Most everything that happens in Audacity takes place on a stage we call the edit window. To understand how Audacity works, we will take the time to examine its interface, including all the controls and buttons.

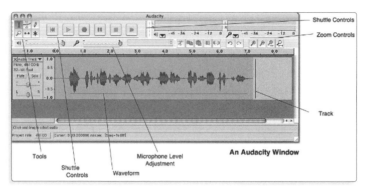

Figure 5.1 Audacity's interface

In the upper left-hand corner of the Audacity window live the six tools. These tools each elicit a different behavior when we click-and-drag around one of the audio tracks. Each time we press the record button, which is positioned with the other shuttle controls, a new track is created. The content recorded on each track can be manipulated independently, so you can adjust where each track begins playback, when one track decreases in volume, and when another begins an increase in volume. As you add more tracks into an Audacity project, you will use the vertical scroll bar to see all of the waveforms that are displayed on each track.

To the right of the shuttle controls (pause, play, stop, reverse, forward, record) are the level meters. These bounce around to indicate the amplitude of the audio signal from the speakers (left) and the microphone (right). Levels should stay in the green zone to avoid clipping or distortion. To the right of the shuttle controls we find the volume and microphone input sliders. We adjust these to control the overall volume of Audacity playback and to adjust the signal's strength from our microphone.

Below the sliders for volume and input levels are several buttons for editing commands (cut, copy, paste) and for changing the resolution of time displayed on the track. Use these to zoom in and zoom out along the timeline.

To the left of each track is an area displaying information about the track, such as the bitrate and frequency. Two sliders accompany each track, as well. The –/+ represents the overall track volume or output, and the L/R slider controls pan. Pan is a description of how far left, center, or right the track appears in the project's stereo image. If we were editing two mono tracks, each representing one person in an interview, we might position one track slightly to the left and the second to the right to create an aural picture of two people talking simultaneously from either side of a room.

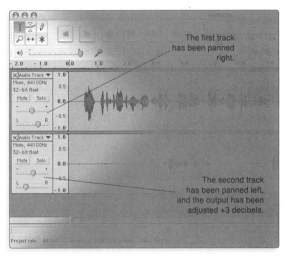

Figure 5.2 By panning each track on different sides of the stereo "image," you can simulate a recording that took place between two people and create a sense of "acoustic" space for a higher-quality podcast.

Edits

Editing digital audio can include a number of transformations, including cuts (removing a portion of a recording), envelope changes (changing some parameter over a period of time), filters (changing the original audio with an effect, such as reverb or echo), and splices (joining two separate chunks together). Editing audio on the Audacity timelines is similar to using a video-editing application, such as Avid, iMovie, or Movie Maker.

To perform edits in Audacity we will use three primary tools: the selection (I-bar) tool, the envelope tool, and the time-shift tool. With the selection tool, you can perform a number of edits. You highlight areas to manipulate on the timeline in the same way you highlight words in a word processor. First, open an audio file, or record something with a microphone into Audacity. Then, select a portion of the waveform on the timeline. With this selection, you can copy or cut, use the delete key, or apply a number of filters under the Effect menu.

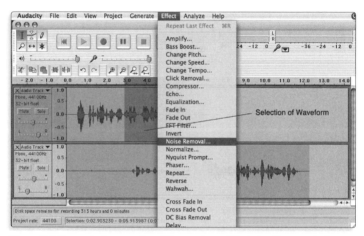

Figure 5.3 Here, selecting a portion of the waveform will limit the effect to only the selected area on the first track.

To change the output (volume) level of a track over time (to fade in or out), we will use the envelope tool. Each click of the envelope tool adds a handle that acts as a point of reference. The next click-and-drag of the mouse (up or down) on the timeline will result in an amplification or decrease in volume in the time period between the two clicks. To perform a slow fade-out, use a greater distance between the two clicks on the timeline.

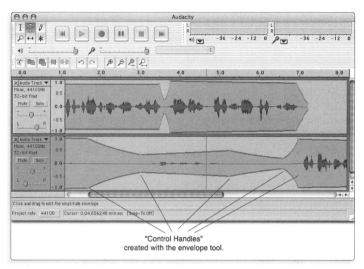

Figure 5.4 Envelope tool

One common edit from raw footage is the removal of mistakes and dead air. Use the selection tool to select areas that need removal, and press the delete or backspace key on the keyboard. To move clips around so that two or more tracks synchronize or line up, use the move tool. Slide the waveform to the left or right to align tracks vertically.

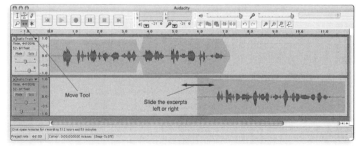

Figure 5.5 Move tool

Many podcasts recorded in Audacity are the result of several takes. Each section in a large podcast project, especially when a podcast includes many students, may require a new take. Each time you press the record button, a new take is created upon a new track. Using the time-shift tool, you can align these takes alongside sound effects or stingers that are added as interstitials in your project. Sound effects can be loaded into your Audacity project by choosing Insert Audio from the Project menu.

Before exporting your Audacity project, listen to the complete edit. Adjust the levels of each track. One useful effect you can apply to tracks with recorded voice is the Compressor. A compression filter reduces the extremes of low and high amplitude (volume) on a track. If you record two folks talking, and one is significantly softer than the other, the Compressor will help raise the softer speaker's volume, making all the voices easier to hear.

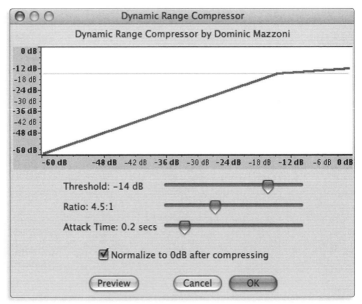

Figure 5.6 Adjust the sliders in the Compressor filter to modify the respective speaker's volume, so the selection is more balanced and easier to hear.

Saving and Exporting

Finally, it is time to save and export your project. (Of course, you should be saving your project throughout the editing process.) When using the File > Save Project command, you are saving it in Audacity's no-compression, project format. When your project is ready for the Web, choose File > Export as MP3. Next, fill out metadata for the MP3 file, including title, artist, and album information, as applicable. For podcasts, the Title should be the title of your podcast episode; the Album, the title of your podcast show. The Artist field can include the host or the podcast producer. Students might use their teacher's or school's name as the artist.

As podcasting emerges as a regular classroom project activity, we will inevitably publish mistakes. "How did I miss that?" a teacher might ask. Fixing editing mistakes is more difficult to do with audio than it is with text and graphics. Digital artists and graphic designers today use Adobe Photoshop to put together complex compositions of type, photography, and digital painting—using layers. These Photoshop layers offer the user control over the various elements that make up one composition, much like the individual tracks in Audacity offer you control when putting together a podcast. In Photoshop, an artist can export everything together as a JPEG file for the Web. We export our podcasts as MP3. In both of these cases, the individual layers and tracks in our respective programs are lost the moment they are exported, making editing of the complex composition nearly impossible. Therefore, just as a graphic designer will keep an archived copy of their original Photoshop file (PSD), complete with all of its original layers, we should keep our original Audacity project files. The length of time the files remain archived is up to you. I recommend at least a school year, if storage space permits. If an edit of your podcast file is required (for whatever reason), the edit will be far simpler to implement by working with the original project file.

ELSEWHERE ON THE WEB

Audacity is a popular program, and there are many online resources to help you and students use it. For starters, here are four:

Official Audacity Tutorials:
http://audacity.sourceforge.net/help/tutorials/

Making a Podcast with Audacity Video:
www.glnd.k12.va.us/podcasts/makingpodcast_audacity3.m4v

Mastering Podcasts with Audacity:
http://software.newsforge.com/article.pl?sid=06/03/17/
1633214&from=rss

Give Your Podcast Professional Polish with Audacity:
www.macworld.com/2005/04/secrets/junecreateside/

Editing with GarageBand

Apple offers several mature, feature-rich programs for creating audio and video podcasts. Among these are GarageBand, iMovie, and Soundtrack Pro. Each of these applications has a focused purpose and is centered around the QuickTime format and its family of file-types: MP3, AAC for audio, and MPEG-4 for video. GarageBand was originally marketed as a music recording and composition tool, but since January of 2006, it has included a podcaster's studio with tools for building enhanced podcasts. These audio podcasts (with an .m4a extension) use AAC compression, but they also embed chapter markers and graphics into the audio file. These have the benefit of playing audio only or audio with PowerPoint-style slides.

iMovie, like Movie Maker or Adobe Premier in Windows, is an ideal tool for creating video podcasts. Soundtrack Pro is a Macintosh-only application for more professional audio editing, and comes bundled with Apple's Final Cut Pro suite for professional video and film editing. Its analogue on the Windows platform is Adobe Audition, which is used heavily by disc jockeys in the radio industry. While I have used a number of these applications to produce composited video podcasts with multiple layers, as well as audio podcasts with multiple tracks and digital effects, GarageBand is a real favorite. It is a valuable tool in any podcaster's toolkit, comes pre-installed on new Apple Macintosh computers, and sells with their iLife suite of applications. Compared with Audacity, it is easier to use and offers many more features, including the attractive ability to build enhanced podcasts.

Once starting GarageBand, it will present a screen for defining what type of project you wish to create. We will choose to create a new podcast.

GarageBand begins each podcasting session with a pre-defined number of tracks. On the left are a podcast track, male voice, female voice, jingles, and radio sounds. More tracks can be added, using the large (+) button further down the interface on the left-hand side.

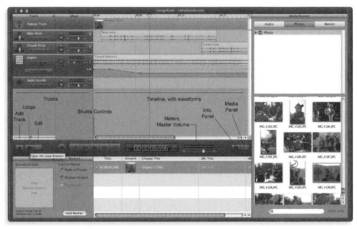

Figure 6.1 GarageBand project creation screen

The podcast track is for building enhanced podcasts. This is where we drag photos into the podcast. Building an enhanced podcast is optional in GarageBand. Each photo dragged into this timeline track defines a new "chapter" in the podcast. These chapters are waypoints through the progression of your project. Listeners to an enhanced podcast can skip ahead by the names you affix to each chapter, much like we do with chapters on a DVD. We will explore enhanced podcasting at the end of our project.

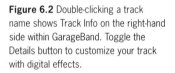

Figure 6.2 Double-clicking a track name shows Track Info on the right-hand side within GarageBand. Toggle the Details button to customize your track with digital effects.

The male and female voice tracks are your main audio tracks. Each has been applied with digital filtering to best complement the male and female voice. If you wish to change the digital enhancement to these tracks, you can change the presets by clicking on the information button ("*i*") on the right-hand side of the interface. For example, you may wish to tweak the settings for two male or three female podcasters.

By keeping different personalities on their own track, editing becomes easier. If you have recorded audio on an external device, such as an iPod with a microphone, and you import the audio into GarageBand, the audio enhancement selected for the track will still improve the sound captured externally. You can easily add WAV files (a common format on external recorders) into GarageBand by dragging the file from the Mac's Finder onto a track within Garage-Band.

The Jingles track within GarageBand is for pre-recorded sound effects, musical introductions, and "bumpers," which are all used to fill in the gaps between podcast segments. You can click on the large "eyeball" icon (left-hand side) to reveal GarageBand's already-installed jingles, or you can use your own jingles through drag-and-drop of an external file.

Finally, the Radio Sounds track is a virtual synthesizer. You cannot drag audio files onto this track. Instead, using a MIDI keyboard, recording on this track remembers what key-presses you "played" on the MIDI keyboard. For this virtual instrument, each key on the keyboard represents a different sound effect (crashes, bells, cymbals). If you do not have a MIDI keyboard connected to your Macintosh, you can use GarageBand's virtual keyboard, which uses some of the letters on your computer keyboard. The sounds heard and recorded on this track are played back by GarageBand's synthesizer engine.

Figure 6.3 Choose Musical Typing from the Window menu in GarageBand to display an alternative to a MIDI keyboard for using Radio Sounds for your podcast.

RECORDING

Before you record using GarageBand, connect any microphone you intend to use. Under GarageBand's preferences, choose your microphone. GarageBand works with USB microphones, such as the popular models from Logitech, Samson, and Blue, as well as digital mixers connected to standard XLR-type microphones. You can also use the built-in microphone on your Macintosh. Using a digital mixer with a FireWire (IEEE-1394) interface, you can also record with more than one microphone at a time, each on its own track. This is called multitrack recording.

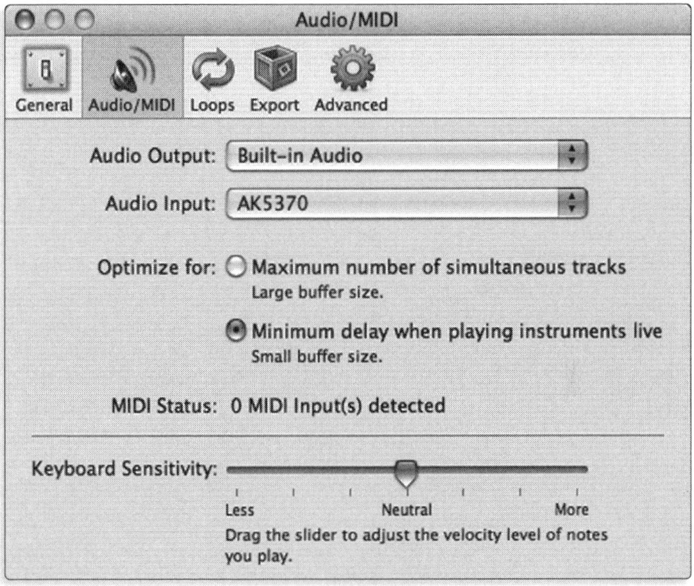

Figure 6.4 Check GarageBand preferences for choosing your input device before attempting to record.

Once your microphone is set up, select the track where you would like audio recorded by clicking on the area around its name and icon. A red dot will appear in the first track button. To enable multiple tracks for multiple-track recording, depress the same track button on alternate tracks. If you are recording and audio already exists on other tracks, GarageBand will playback these tracks while you record a new one. Because you do not want the microphone to pick up audio from previously recorded tracks, either mute the pre-recorded tracks with the second track button (mute) or use headphones. Conversely, you can also automatically mute all other tracks by depressing the third button: solo.

Next to each track are mixer controls for adjusting pan (how far left or right the track appears in the stereo image), volume, and ducking. Above each volume slider are level meters that bounce as the audio plays back on each track. A master volume control and level meter is located center-right in the GarageBand interface. The ducking arrows (up-yellow, down-blue) control automatic-level adjustment between tracks.

Figure 6.5 Track and Mixing controls offer fine-tuned control over each track in GarageBand. Under the tracks, mute and solo are helpful in isolating the playback of fewer tracks. Under the mixer, the knobs control pan, and the sliders control volume.

By default, the Jingles track in GarageBand is ducked down, and the two voice tracks are ducked up. Ducking only affects tracks where the buttons are illuminated blue and yellow. The "down" track will automatically "duck out of the way" when audio is present on the "up" track. If you use introductory music on the Jingle track and then begin your podcast on the voice track, the music on the Jingles track will automatically decrease (duck) in volume when speaking begins. In Audacity, or earlier versions of GarageBand, you would have to do this manually.

Each track in GarageBand can still be manually controlled for volume and pan. The last track button (a down-pointing arrow for each track) reveals envelope controls. Points may be clicked on the envelope line underneath each track for controlling volume and pan over time. If you wanted to separate two speakers sharing one microphone, for instance, you could manually adjust pan left and pan right for each respective speaker. Adjusting volume will allow you to manually do a fade-in or fade-out.

Figure 6.6 Envelope control appears below each track when toggled with the triangle under each track's name, left. You can add as many control points as you like along the line for volume or pan.

The shuttle controls (record, play, rewind, fast-forward), located center, control movement of the playhead. Anytime during playback or recording, you can use the spacebar to start or stop playback. You can also use the "R" key on the keyboard to begin recording on the selected track. Before recording, test the level output of your microphone so the sound is loud enough (green zone), but not too loud (yellow-red) using your track's level meter.

EDITING

Editing in GarageBand is a simple process of sliding sound clips left, right, and between audio tracks, and then making cuts or splices. You can edit completely on the timeline, or you can use the track editor to fine-tune your edits. You can toggle the track editor with the scissors button, located center-left.

Within the track editor, use the mouse cursor to make selections. Typically, this is used to make a precise selection of where you will make a cut, by pressing the delete key. Clicking and dragging at the beginning of a clip on the main timeline or the track editor will move the clip left or right. Clicking and dragging at the end will allow you to repeat the same clip, over and over. While repeating an audio clip with voice is not common, repeating Jingle materials and percussion tracks for transitional or background sound is.

You can toggle the lower portion of the GarageBand window by pressing the eye/loop button, located center-left. Loops are pre-recorded sound bites, organized into jingles, stingers, and sound effects. Click on individual loops to hear a preview. In the listing of loops, you will find columns showing a loop's length and a column for marking the loop as a favorite. You may elect to first listen to a variety of loops and jingles, and then mark favorites. Your favorites are then listed under the Favorites category in the loops column.

Figure 6.7 Search the loops browser for royalty-free musical excerpts to use in your podcast production.

TRACK SETTINGS

Each track in GarageBand has a number of settings, including which digital effects are applied. Toggle the Details triangle in the track information panel to add digital effects and customize the sound on a per-track basis. Using these controls, you can also record voice tracks in mono, versus stereo. If you are not using a stereo microphone, and you want to separate the channels between two or more tracks, recording in mono will save resources in your recording project. Under Track Information, you can also turn on track monitoring, which will playback the audio from the microphone to your headphones. This will enable you to hear what the recorded sound—including the digital processing of effects—will sound like. Do not use this feature with conventional speakers, as you will create a feedback loop.

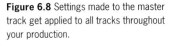

Figure 6.8 Settings made to the master track get applied to all tracks throughout your production.

Under MasterTrack, you can make adjustments that get applied to the entire podcast project, including the amount of ducking that GarageBand automatically applies to tracks.

ENHANCED PODCASTING

With GarageBand 3, Apple added support for enhanced podcasts. Using the podcast track, you can enhance podcasts by splitting them up into chunks called "chapters" and assign a title, a Web URL, and a photograph for each chapter. While you can drag a Quick-Time movie to the podcast track, you cannot mix both pictures and movies. Dragging a movie to this top track will convert your GarageBand podcast into a movie with a soundtrack. I recommend using iMovie, instead, for creating video podcasts.

To get started with the podcast track, reveal the media browser by clicking on the media button (center right). GarageBand reveals the content already stored in your iTunes, iPhoto, and movies folder. If you have already prepared photos for use in your podcast with iPhoto, they will be here, ready to drag into the podcast track. With the latest version of GarageBand, Apple now supports media from their professional photography application Aperture, from within the media browser.

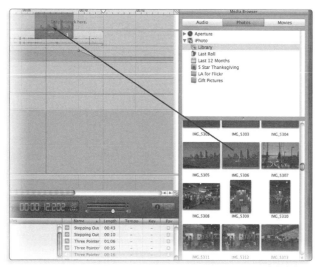

Figure 6.9 To create an enhanced podcast, drag photos from your iPhoto or Aperture collections into the first track in GarageBand (version 3 or later).

Toggling the track editor again (scissors icon) will reveal the chapter times, titles, and Web addresses. The precise location where you drop photos in the podcast track will determine where each chapter is made. You can adjust these later by dragging the end of a clip left or right, or by editing the precise number in the track editor.

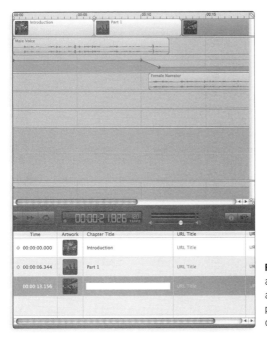

Figure 6.10 The titles added for each chapter appear alongside the podcast track's picture on the top.

You can create as many chapters as you like, but only chapters with titles will appear as chapters when played back in iTunes or on the QuickTime Player. Students may use the URL attribute of each chapter to point to areas of interest or research when putting together a podcast project. Teachers may use the URL chapter attribute to point listeners to the school's or teacher's own Web site. An overlay with the Web URL or Web site title will appear within the podcast at playback time, and it is an authentic, clickable link. Where QuickTime is installed, exported, enhanced podcasts can be watched (including support for chapters and Web links) on both Macs and PCs.

SHARING/EXPORTING

Like a project file in Audacity, your GarageBand project is a master file that is easy to update and edit later. Keep a copy of your project for as long as you can. To publish a podcast, choose Share > Export Podcast to Disk. This will compress all the tracks, add the images, and prepare the audio podcast. When the export process is complete, transfer your file to a Web server for sharing.

Apple includes support for their ".Mac" service (a subscription account that comes with e-mail and additional services within several of their iLife programs), including GarageBand. By choosing Share > Export to iWeb, GarageBand does more toward getting your podcast published. When using iWeb, another iLife application, posting podcasts, blogs, and photos online takes just a few clicks. iWeb also handles publishing an RSS feed and transferring your content to Apple's ".Mac" servers.

CHAPTER 7
Blogging

As with many worthwhile pursuits in life, to understand blogging you must participate. At its core, of course, blogging is writing. More than that, it is a genre of writing that can accommodate a variety of writing styles. Yet all blogs share unique characteristics: Blogs are organized into short posts, appear as an ongoing collection of posts in reverse chronological order, and often include interactive elements, such as trackbacks and comments. Once you have established a blog, maintaining it is easy—just write! In this chapter we will examine how to start the process by looking at both reading and writing blogs, and by looking at many of the blogging software choices.

Choosing a blogging system, sometimes called a "platform," is like choosing a new car. We likely lack the experience of one brand over another, and on the surface, they can all lure us with their respective bells and whistles. For educators, choosing a good blogging platform can be the difference between smart integration of Read/Write Web technology and a big mistake. The choice is more difficult when we consider the fact that some platforms are free and open-source, while others demand a purchase price, and still others require the hardware and technical support necessary to support a blogging initiative. Let me help you wade through the choices.

OPEN-SOURCE OPTIONS

Among the popular open-source options are blojsom, Blosxom, WordPress, and Textpattern. The list changes daily, of course, because there is always a newcomer offering easier installation, better support, and more attractive features. Open Source CMS (www.opensourcecms.com) offers working-demo previews of many popular platforms, including access to the administrative screens and controls. No matter which you choose, the open-source solutions have some similarities we will consider.

First, open-source software is free to use, but many times lacks traditional avenues of support. If you have trouble with the software, there is no one to call to fix it. Instead, running open-source software requires personnel with the expertise to install, backup, and troubleshoot the software.

Second, open-source software needs a Web server to run on—either your own server hosted at your school or district, or a hosted server. Hosting companies offer monthly fees for holding your content. In some cases, they are a good solution when running open-source software. The better hosting outfits offer easy-to-use, push-button installers. They likely have also chosen the blogging software that requires the least amount of intervention from their tech-support staff, too.

Third, using open-source software is part of a forward-thinking trend, one that seems to be growing in popularity with each passing day. When choosing the more popular platforms, you will find communities of users who are willing to assist one another through online forums and mailing lists. Open-source software is typically first to enjoy faster, cutting-edge features, and (when well supported) it benefits from quick updates and bug fixes.

Apple bundles the free blojsom engine (based on the Java/Tomcat Web server platform) with their OS X Tiger server product. When you buy an Apple server, an unlimited client version of the software is included, which comes with blojsom. You can also install a newer version of blojsom yourself on any platform. For simple blogging, it is an easy platform to administer with Apple's server administration tools. It also supports podcast publishing, complete with support for RSS.

Blosxom is the earlier version of blojsom and is special among blogging platforms. It does not offer every bell and whistle, but it is easy to install. Blosxom uses simple text files (uploaded to a server) as the basis for blog management. It uses the timestamp on each file to organize the blog in reverse chronological order. Publishing your blog is as easy as saving an ASCII text file to a server. Unlike the solutions that follow, there is no database to set up and configure.

WordPress and Textpattern both enjoy popularity, with WordPress currently in the lead. Both require the PHP scripting language and MySQL database, two more open-source tools. WordPress offers a free service at www.wordpress.com, where they will host your WordPress-based blog for you. As more bloggers are using these platforms, you are likely to enjoy more support with installation and maintenance.

With the exception of blojsom (as Apple bundles it with Mac OS X Tiger Server), all these open-source platforms support a one-blog approach. If, for instance, you want to use WordPress to manage a school Web site or to set up a classroom blog where 90 students and 2 teachers will participate, this one-blog scenario works fine; if, however, you want each teacher or each student to maintain their own blog, it does not.

There are two solutions for hosting multiple-blog versions of WordPress. Two sites—WordPress.com and EduBlogs—each use the same engine, WordPress MU (http://mu.wordpress.org). The "MU" stands for "multiple users." Another, run by ibiblio, is Lyceum (http://lyceum.ibiblio.org), also based on WordPress. You may wish to use these free services to host your blogs on the WordPress platform, or you may want to use Lyceum or WordPress MU on your own server. Be prepared either way, as you will need unique e-mail addresses for each student or teacher who participates.

Moodle (http://moodle.org) is an open-source course management system. Moodle's installation proves a challenge for some and requires PHP, the open-source Apache Web server, as well as a database such as MySQL. It is specifically geared toward educational applications, and with version 1.6 (and later), it offers blogs. Moodle's blogs are not as robust and interactive as the others listed here, but they are presented as an integrated part of the Moodle course system. With credentials required to enter your Moodle server, it can be a more secure solution for blogging students.

Yet another popular system that's more than just being about blogs is Drupal (http://drupal.org). Drupal is a content management system for running an entire Web site, but it also includes blogs. Drupal runs on a variety of platforms and Web servers and includes other collaborative features, such as discussion forums and a built-in Web-based news aggregator.

FREE, BUT NOT OPEN-SOURCE

Next for consideration are blogging platforms that do not live on our own servers. We have already considered WordPress.com. EduBlogs offers a similar type of service for techers and students. Blogger.com, one of the original sites that has brought push-button publishing to the masses, is free. Blogger can be used to publish content on your own server, but it can also be used with Google's free BlogSpot hosting, so that both the blog and the software that runs it is out of your hands.

Many students use social networks such as MySpace (www.myspace. com) and Facebook (www.facebook.com) that both offer services similar to blogging. Another popular site with students is Live-Journal (www.livejournal.com), offering socialization features as well. Six Apart, the company that previously ran LiveJournal, also started Vox (www.vox.com), a new service built around a community concept. All of these choices are free. Some have restrictions on age, and some make it easier than others for other users to discover your real identity, so read their service agreements carefully.

PAID BLOGGING SERVICES AND PLATFORMS

Finally, we come to blogging that costs money. In this category, there are a number of solutions, from those that echo the complications of the open-source experience to those that make starting a blog painless. First, we consider Expression Engine (http://expressionengine. com). Expression Engine is a versatile content management system that supports the concept of a blog. (I say "concept" because the database-driven design of its Web page templates does not have to be a blog.) Expression Engine easily handles multiple users, multiple blogs, and different roles that can be assigned to each user.

TypePad (www.typepad.com) is another Six Apart-branded blogging system that is easy to set up and is hosted on their servers. TypePad supports one blogger or multiple bloggers on a tiered-payment scheme, depending on your space and flexibility requirements. TypePad is likely an easy system to use for an organization where no plans to host or maintain your own server exist. Unlike the free Blogger service, your entire TypePad blogs can live at one domain name without having your own server to manage.

If TypePad sounds attractive, but you do not mind hosting blogs yourself on your own local or shared server, consider Movable Type (www.movabletype.com), the premier blogging solution from Six Apart. Before becoming eclipsed by WordPress, Movable Type was one of the most popular blogging platforms, and it still enjoys wide support. Their enterprise edition can manage thousands of bloggers, and it offers the ability to make customized templates. It will also e-mail visitors to blogs when updates are published.

Another well-regarded platform called Community Server (http:// communityserver.org) offers both server software that you install yourself, as well as a hosted solution (http://communityserver.com). This solution is ideal for its robust management controls and is ideally suited to organizations dependent on Microsoft IIS Web server.

THINGS TO CONSIDER

With so many choices available today for providing blogging services to educators and students, what's best? I am not sure any perfect solution exists. The platforms such as Expression Engine, Movable Type, and Community Server that you pay for and install on your own hardware offer the desirable control over your own content, the polish of a professional-level Web application, and flexibility in determining the look, fit, and finish of your blogging Web site.

Other solutions such as the Apple-modified blojsom (with OS X Tiger Server) and the WordPress blogs let you control who reads your blogs. You can restrict readership to approved parties only. When you introduce blogging to students, you also have to consider what control you want for disabling blogs or changing a blog's content, in the event students (or anyone else in your organization) violate your acceptable use policy. Some systems do a better job than others in controlling both aspects of access: access by blog authors and by blog readers.

Educators may also consider not opening their blogging projects to the world. Instead, you may prefer hosting your own blogs on an intranet—a local network that is not accessible to anyone outside of the school. Another solution is to open access to blogs to the world, but to require password authentication to get to that area of the server that hosts the blogs.

Blogging in schools today has exciting prospects. Do not let all the decisions and considerations involved in choosing *how* to get started stop you or slow you down. Make a good, educated guess, by weighing costs and the technical expertise required and available, and then start with a limited number of bloggers. Whether you choose the education-centered blogs that come with a Moodle course system that you host on your own server, or you choose the free "on your own" style from Blogger.com, remember the very act of blogging encourages writing, organization, communication, and collaboration. Blogging is at the heart of the Read/Write Web. Blogging can give each student a voice and can also bring students together through the various levels of linking inherent in a blog's comments and trackbacks.

Writing Blogs: *Planning*

Once you have chosen a platform to use for blogging, there are still choices to be made. What will you blog about? How frequently will you blog? If it is someone else blogging—what content, guidelines, and frequency will shape their experience? When we ask students to blog, there are other things to consider about what they will write. As an instructor, you may ask them to write about their reflections on a reading. But can they also write about other topics of interest? Should a blogging teacher be discouraged from sharing aspects of his or her personal life (e.g., family vacations)? How might administrators define the lines between professional and personal blogging? These issues should be considered by educators before embarking on the blog bandwagon. An Acceptable Use Policy (AUP) should guide some of these issues, but the goals of blogging—whether it be for increasing school-home communication or serving as a forum for students to write about what they are learning—ought to dictate not only how often we write, but what we write, and how *what* is written is assessed and judged.

Writing Blogs: *Reading and More Reading*

A common experience encountered when assigning blogging assignments, which teachers often cite to me, is becoming overwhelmed with what they have to read! "Blogging can take a lot out of me!" said one inundated teacher. While the blogs that students write do need to be monitored, assessed, and considered as part of their educational experience, creating blogging buddies, encouraging peer feedback, and asking students to present (for a grade) only their best blogging work can help lessen the burden of reading so many student blogs.

By publishing student blogs online, teachers can also take advantage of connected parents and invite them into the experience. When community members and parents participate in the blogging by writing comments and offering feedback for the students, it offers the students an audience for their writing. In this way, "blogging as technology" helps extend the learning community with which students participate. RSS plays an important role in blogging by keeping everyone up-to-date with the content. It's part of what makes this form of communication so powerful.

Writing Blogs: *Offline, Online*

Using blogs on the Web requires access to the Internet, and if we are adding pictures and audio content to our blogs, we need high-speed access. Yet, everyone does not yet have access to affordable, high-speed Internet service, or anytime/anywhere access to a device that gets us online. The typical way to begin writing a blog is to go to the Web site that runs the blog software (e.g., Blogger.com, our own installation of WordPress MU, or our TypePad account), login, come up with a title, and then supply the body, or post, of our writing. In this model, because we have to stay connected the entire time (from login to finishing our entire post), blog posts tend to be short and informal. So where might we turn if we need more time to compose more thoughtful posts, or more flexibility to compose a post offline, and then time-delay its publication?

A new class of desktop application, called the "blog editor," has emerged and is dedicated to offline blog composition. Even the latest version of Microsoft Word for Windows Vista supports blog editing. The offline editor periodically "talks" with your online blog. You compose the title and the blog entry; you assign the categories and tags; import the photos; and work for as long as you like in this specialized editing application. When you are prepared to publish your post, you press the requisite button and the software uploads the new post, its date, and all the accoutrements. In short, a blog editor offers a richer editing experience on the desktop, independent of the Web browser.

Popular blog editors include:

- BlogJet (Windows)—http://blogjet.com

- ecto (Windows, Macintosh)—http://ecto.kung-foo.tv

- Performancing Firefox extension (Windows, Macintosh)—http://performancing.com/firefox/

- w.bloggar (Windows)—http://wbloggar.com

- MarsEdit (Macintosh)—www.red-sweater.com/marsedit/

Among these solutions, w.bloggar for Windows and the Performancing extension for Firefox are free.

Blog editors can make the task of blogging a lot more dynamic and fun by making the process of publishing even easier. In schools, they can become part of a blogging practice that involves teacher approval before student blog posts are published. The same advice holds true here as it does for choosing a blogging platform: evaluate, test, and "kick the tires" to see what will support the goals for blogging in your school.

LET'S BLOG

WordPress

Since so many solutions are available for publishing content to a blog, I have chosen to take you step-by-step through the blogging process for WordPress, one of the blogging solutions mentioned in this chapter. It is flexible and offers a lot of control for who reads what (blog authors can assign a per-post password required for access), as well as control for choosing engaging blog templates (Web page designs around your content). Once WordPress is set up on your server, the maintenance burden is on the users to manage comments, trackbacks, and the look of their blogs.

To get started, point your browser to your WordPress login screen. This login area is likely at your site's domain name–slash [/]–"wp-admin." Once you provide the correct username and password, you will encounter the WordPress Dashboard. Depending on your level of access, you control everything here, including removing comments, authoring new posts, or configuring any number of plugins that extend the functionality of your blog.

Click on Write at the top-left to begin writing a new blog post. A new screen appears, a virtual blank slate. First, provide a blog post title. The title is important: it should well-reflect what you are writing about. "This week's homework" would be a poor choice if your blog

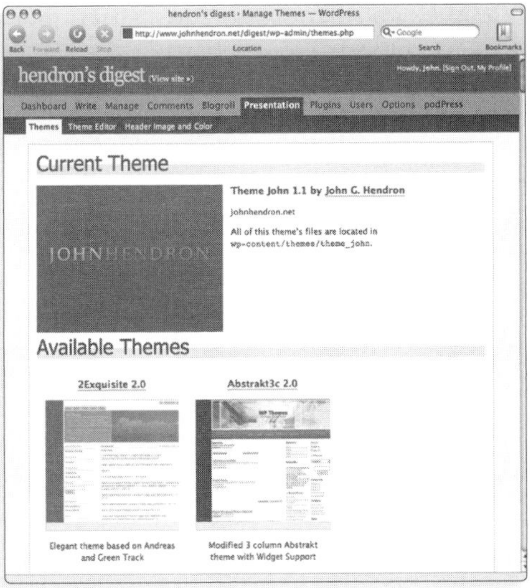

Figure 7.1 Because blogs work by dynamically presenting database-stored content into a Web page template, many blog systems, including WordPress (pictured here), can easily change the look of your Web site by changing to a different template. With WordPress, you can customize these templates yourself or use one designed by other WordPress bloggers. The screenshots here are from my own professional Web site, johnhendron.net. Installation of WordPress was simple, thanks to a one-click installer provided by my Web hosting company. Note the main menu choices within WordPress: Dashboard, Write, Manage, and Comments.

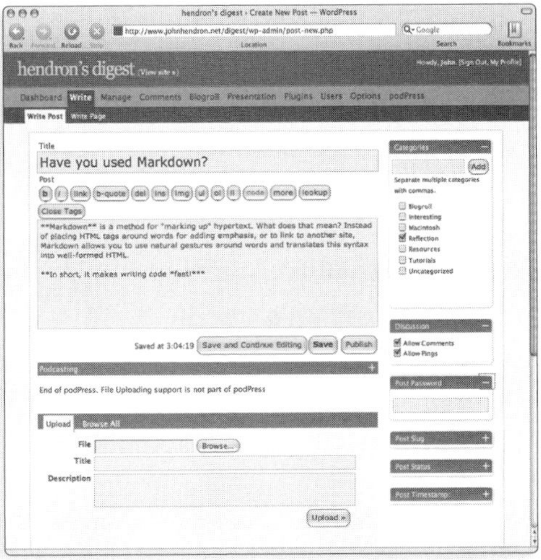

Figure 7.2 Using Markdown is easy once you learn some basic formatting syntax. In this example, double-asterisks (**) around text makes it bold, and a single asterisk (*) around text makes it italic. Markdown can be used to form bulleted lists, create links, and insert images. The Podcasting area seen here is from an additional plugin, called PodPress.

posts commonly listed homework assignments. Two months from now, what would this mean in a sea of homework blog posts?

Next, write your content. Since WordPress supports multiple plugin systems for simplifying the markup of your content, I will use a popular syntax called Markdown, enabled through the Markdown plugin (www.michelf.com). Markdown generates XHTML-compliant code for bold text, hyperlinks, and anything else you can do with HTML. Learning Markdown syntax takes time, but it is powerful, and it's easier than writing HTML. Conversely, you will notice editing buttons above the Post area that can be used to assist in the insertion of HTML tags.

When writing for WordPress, separate paragraphs with double carriage returns. To insert a media file, such as a JPEG image, use the Upload area below the post field to upload a local file on your computer to the server. Provide both a title and a description, as these files can be used in future blog posts, too, by clicking on Browse All. By clicking the Send to Editor command (near the thumbnail picture that appears with your JPEG image in the Upload area), WordPress will insert the appropriate tag for displaying an image.

Figure 7.3 Scroll down when editing a post to reveal an image-upload area in WordPress. Other sections, expanded by clicking the plus (+), reveal trackbacks, excerpts for the RSS feed, and the use of custom fields required for some plugins.

An optional excerpt can be added to your post that will appear in the RSS newsfeed that WordPress generates. Some bloggers encourage visits to their sites by providing short teasers rather than all the content in the feed. The choice is yours. The choice is likewise yours to deny comments (discussion), password-protect your individual post, assign a category for organizational purposes, change the time the post shows published (post timestamp), and more.

Finally, click on the Publish button and your blog post goes live. Publishing a blog post is a concise, focused operation that separates the look of the complete blog from its content. In essence, we have added new content to the blog's database, and the next time someone visits the blog, the WordPress software fetches the content, plugs it into the template file we have chosen already, and organizes our content on the page by the timestamps assigned to each post.

Clicking the Manage tab at the top of our WordPress system will display a list of the last fifteen posts. We can view the titles, the assigned categories, the authors, and the number of comments

Figure 7.4 The Manage screen in WordPress shows the last 15 posts. You can search for older posts to edit, view, or delete them. To manage comments left by visitors, go to the separate Comments screen.

made on each post. View/Edit/Delete buttons for each post sit to the right-hand side of the page; Edit allows us to make changes to an already-published post. Any unpublished, saved posts will appear above the list, under Drafts.

WordPress and WordPress MU are powerful blogging systems that make publishing to our blog easy, through a Web browser or dedicated blog editor. Next, let us look at publishing to a WordPress blog using ecto, a popular blog editor for both Macintosh and Windows.

ecto

The first time you run ecto, you will follow a series of on-screen boxes asking for information about your blog. Because you will be composing and publishing blog entries off your desktop instead of your browser, ecto needs to know how to communicate with your blog. Each blogging system has its own way of accepting input and output from these blog-editing applications.

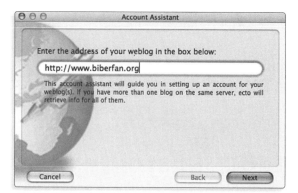

Figure 7.5 The first step in setting up ecto to publish your blog is to provide the domain name of your blog. This should point to the front page of your blog.

Next, ecto visits your blog and tries to figure out what type of blog system you are using. In my case, it correctly determined I am using WordPress. If your blog editor does not guess so well, check the documentation of both your software and blog editor to find the right match.

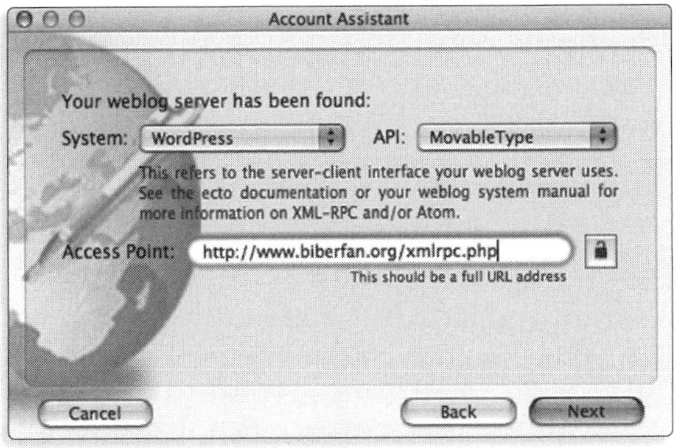

Figure 7.6 WordPress uses the standard interface (established by Movable Type) for connecting to off-server editors such as ecto. The XML-RPC file is what processes the communication between my blog and my copy of ecto.

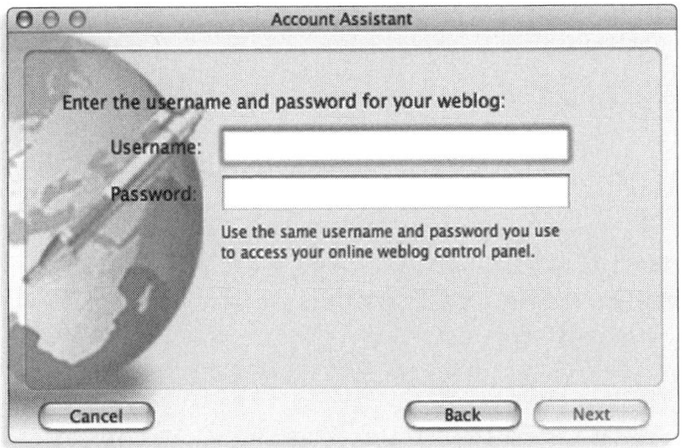

Figure 7.7 If you forget your username and password, but can still access your blog through the Web, visit the Users section in Word-Press and reset your password. WordPress will also give you the option to reset your password by sending e-mail to your account. This is one reason blogging systems such as WordPress require unique e-mail addresses for each user.

The next step in setting up ecto is to provide credentials. Here, provide the username and password you established when setting up your blog. Any username from your membership of bloggers who are connected with your blog can be used here.

ecto's Account Assistant asks us for default settings. These settings become the "standard" each time we author a new blog post. Allow Comments sets the default comment capability. Trackbacks allow others to drop links from your blog post into their site. "Notify weblog directories" sends a message to online services telling them "your blog has fresh content." Web search engines use this data to index your site, making it easier for other users to find your content. For student blogs on the Internet, I recommend turning it off. For blogs on an intranet, it should also be disabled.

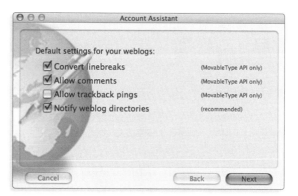

Figure 7.8 Because of a problem called "comment spam," many bloggers today choose not to allow comments on every single post. Comments can be turned off or on for each post but the Account Assistant defines the default comments-capability.

Next, ecto will "talk" to your blog and download what you may or may not have already written. You can organize your list of entries by title, date, or category. When you click on entries in your list, the content will be displayed in the lower-half of the window.

Figure 7.9 ecto's interface is not too different from an e-mail application or news aggregator.

Figure 7.10 ecto offers two modes for editing: the HTML mode seen here, and a rich-text mode that works more like a word processor, with easy support for changing text formatting and importing graphics. The tools, buttons, and options around the blog post extend ecto's usefulness by offering the blogger more fine-tuned control over every aspect of the blog post.

Double-clicking an already-authored post will allow you to edit it. Clicking the New Post button will open a blank window for editing.

Once your editing is complete, you can use the Save command to save your post locally on your computer's hard drive. If you only have limited access to the Internet, this allows you to author blog posts anytime and publish them later through ecto (or any desktop blogging editor) when you connect to the Internet. The Publish button saves the entry and sends it directly to your blog.

BLOGGING AND PODCASTING

Blogging enables us to quickly get content on the Web. (Blogging editor applications are even emerging for handheld devices and so-called smart phones.) With just an Internet connection, we can establish a blog for free and begin to publish content. Blog content is not only read but is also interactive, through trackbacks to a reader's blog or through comments left to extend the conversation. Blogs can also be used to publish podcasts. In the chapters on Audacity and GarageBand, we looked at how to record and edit content. In this section, we will use the free Blogger.com platform and another free Web site, FeedBurner, to publish an RSS 2.0, podcast-capable newsfeed. To create multimedia content that others can subscribe to, we use a blog's automatic ability to create RSS newsfeeds.

Some weblogs support podcast publishing without help from FeedBurner. If your blog does not support RSS attachments, this method will convert Atom and RSS 1.0 feeds into the RSS 2.0–flavor required for podcasting. Publishing with Blogger and FeedBurner is a multi-step process:

1. Create a free Blogger.com blog. If you have a Google Account, setting up a blog is simple. Go to www.blogger.com and sign in. You can also create a new

Google Account from the Blogger homepage. A good name for this blog is the title of your podcast.

2. Upload your podcast file to a Web server. You will need some space online to host your podcast. If it is a popular podcast, check bandwidth requirements. Options include a school server that is accessible on the Internet or a Web space provided by a Web site hosting company. Your Internet service provider (ISP) may also have space available for free.

3. From the Blogger Dashboard, create a new post in Blogger. Describe the podcast in the blog entry space, and then link to the podcast file. The link can use the HTML for a hyperlink (e.g., <a href="[…]">Listen to this podcast</a>), or it can use the link button in Blogger's blog composition toolbar. The title of your blog post should be the title of your podcast episode. Publish the blog entry.

4. Copy your blog's newsfeed URL (Blogger newsfeeds appear in this format: http://*yourblogname*.blogspot. com/feeds/posts/default). Copy the URL where you see a Subscribe to Posts link on your blog.

5. Go to FeedBurner.com. Paste your newsfeed URL into FeedBurner, below the invitation to Start FeedBurning now.

6. Check the I am Podcaster! option before clicking Next. In the next screen, sign up for a FeedBurner account (if you do not already have one).

7. Copy-paste the new FeedBurner-created RSS newsfeed into a safe place: this is your podcast newsfeed.

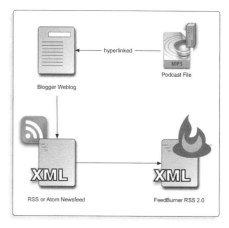

Figure 7.11 The method used here uses two services to publish a podcast. Visitors can use the Blogger blog to read more about the podcast episodes, or use the FeedBurner newsfeed to subscribe.

While we went through several steps to get started with publishing podcasts through a blog, in the future you will go through only two primary steps in publishing new podcasts. First, you will upload the podcast file to a server; second, you'll write a new blog post that includes a link to the podcast file. The RSS newsfeeds will automatically be updated.

Alternatively, for a fee, there are easier solutions for publishing your podcast files. Libsyn Pro (http://libsynpro.com) is a subscription service that hosts your podcast files and creates RSS feeds. This is a good solution for a school where access to space on a Web server for publishing podcasts does not exist.

CHAPTER 8

Using News Aggregators

News aggregators, readers, feed-readers, and the like, are applications that decode RSS and translate it into individual blog entries, news stories, or otherwise logical chunks of information. There are currently three varieties of news aggregators: desktop-based aggregators, Web-based aggregators, and integrated aggregators. The last is the newest breed: Web browsers and other applications that include embedded news-reading capabilities. Popular browsers such as Opera and Safari on the Macintosh and Internet Explorer 7 (IE 7) on Microsoft Windows now aggregate RSS newsfeeds. Even Mozilla Firefox includes a version of RSS support called Live Bookmarks. Each type of aggregator, you might gather, has its advantages.

Desktop aggregators keep your newsfeeds organized in one, central location. They are highly configurable but require a regular connection to the Internet to check the status of your subscribed feeds. Web-based aggregators are a great choice for folks who work on multiple computers or platforms. No matter where you last read your newsfeeds, you can log in on any computer with Internet access and get to your current cache of read and un-read news. Finally, the embedded news aggregators are convenient. When you are browsing the Web, you do not have to switch applications when clicking on one of those XML badges. Browser-based aggregators do not yet have all the controls their desktop counterparts do, but they do enable you to get started with RSS right away.

In this chapter, we will look at three different scenarios in using a news aggregator. We will track 1) student blogs with a desktop-based aggregator, 2) personal and professional blogs with a Web-based aggregator, and 3) school-published newsfeeds with the aggregator embedded in our browser.

TRACKING MY BLOGGING STUDENTS: DESKTOP AGGREGATOR

Whether you are tracking student blogs as part of a lesson where blogging plays an integral role in the learning process (examples of which are included within this book) or simply as an aid in student productivity, the instructor will need to routinely monitor what students are posting in their blogs. For this example, using Net-NewsWire (www.ranchero.com) for Macintosh, let us assume you are an instructor with 120 students, spread across four classes, and you have assigned each student a blog housed on your school-based server. The particulars about the blogging platform are not important here, nor is the type of server that is being used (let's assume, however, your school is using Movable Type on a Windows-based server). What is important is that the server is not "live" on the Internet. Instead, it is behind the school's firewall, and it is only accessible on the school's intranet.

Because your server is not on the Internet, an application-based aggregator like NetNewsWire is the best choice. While you, the instructor, are at school, you can allow the aggregator to check for new blog posts throughout the day. Live-checking will not be available once you leave the building. This is why a Web-based aggregator will not work. While the examples that follow illustrate the use of NetNewsWire, the procedure we follow is almost identical when using other desktop-based aggregators, including NewsGator Feed-Demon (www.newsgator.com) for Windows, Sharp Reader (www.sharpreader.net) for Windows, or RSS Reader (www.rssreader.com) for Windows.

Step 1: *Set Up Your Groups*

The better aggregators allow us to group our newsfeed subscriptions into groups or categories. NetNewsWire (NNW) calls these groups. Through the File menu, we will choose New Group to create groups for each of our classes. We will create a group for each class. The groups appear as folders on the sidebar within NNW.

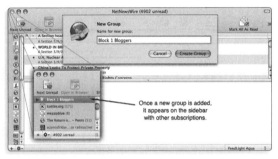

Figure 8.1 Creating a group or folder inside a news aggregator helps keep subscriptions organized.

Step 2: *Hunt Your Newsfeeds*

Next, we need to find the newsfeeds we want to subscribe to. Within Mac OS X, Apple's Safari browser contains a preference option for your preferred news aggregator. By default, it is Safari (version 2 or higher). If you need to, change Safari's preference to NNW before

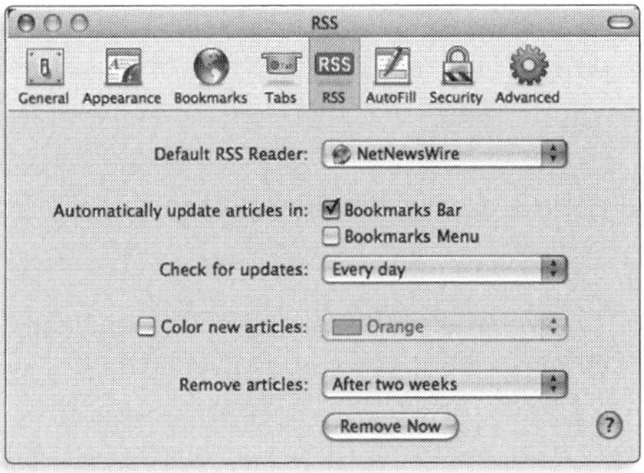

Figure 8.2 Settings for choosing a default news aggregator will vary between the programs and operating system you use.

subscribing to your classes' blogs. If you are using Internet Explorer 6 (or lower) on a Windows PC, you will be copying/pasting the feed URLs into your news aggregator.

Step 3: *Click on the RSS/XML Links*

Now, using Safari, we will browse to each student's blog. Doing this 120 times is a lot of clicking, but rest assured, we only need to do it once. Because our example blogging platform, Movable Type, includes the RSS feed links on each blog, we click each RSS link, and NNW accepts each subscription. Click OK within NNW to accept the subscription, and then go back to Safari to add yet another blog.

Figure 8.3 Once you click on an RSS link from Safari, NetNewsWire picks up the subscription. Click Subscribe to confirm.

Step 4: *Group Them Together*

After subscribing to our student blogs, it will be a simple task of dragging those individual blogs listed in the sidebar into the group folders we create. If you visit the student blogs class by class, between each class subscription, re-visit NNW and drag those individual blog subscriptions within the group folders we created. When you view the subscribed blog posts in NNW, you can do so within each group. NNW lets you browse through each feed individually, or through the whole group together when the folder is selected.

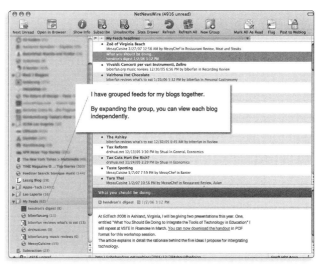

Figure 8.4 While not a class in this picture, I have created a group to collect my own feeds from various blog projects. It is always a good idea to test your feeds to make sure they are working before distributing them to others.

Step 5: *Decide How Often You Will Check*

Visit the NNW preferences to choose how often NNW checks for newsfeed updates off your server. There are two places to make this setting. First, you can set a default choice in Preferences > Downloading > Feeds. Typically, a setting that checks once per day is a good choice. The more often you check for feed updates, the more taxed the Web server is. If you are checking your own server only, you may wish to choose something more frequent, such as every 30 minutes. You can also set the checking frequency for each group, independent of the setting made in preferences.

Exit the NNW preferences, choose one of your group folders within the sidebar, and choose Window > Info. Under Refreshing, choose the update frequency for this group. You may wish to update your Web-based feeds every 4 hours and your student blog feeds every hour, for example. Repeat the Info on each group you monitor to set the refresh schedule.

Figure 8.5 With NetNewsWire, you can change the refresh schedule on individual feeds, or by any group of feeds.

Once all your classroom blog newsfeeds are added into NNW, NNW will begin checking the feeds for updates on a regular basis. New, unread blog posts will appear in bold. The number of unread blog posts is displayed in the application's title bar and in the applications dock icon. For NNW to continuously check newsfeeds, leave it running in the background on your computer. It only checks feeds when it is running. Because NNW downloads the content from blogs to your computer, you can still read the newsfeeds later, when you are off the school network. NNW cannot check for updates, but it will allow you to read the blog posts offline, much like like reading e-mail.

By no means is this an exhaustive look at NetNewsWire. Some of NNW's features are Mac-only, such as its ability to read-back blog posts with computerized speech, or its ability to quickly search blog posts using OS X Spotlight technology. Like NewsGator's Windows counterpart, FeedDemon, NNW allows you to synchronize what you have read with NewsGator's servers. If you have multiple copies of NNW on different computers, this is a great convenience. In this example, however, it will not help us unless you access multiple computers behind your school's firewall.

Step 6: *Happy Reading*

No matter what students are publishing in their blogs—literature reviews in English, lab reports in science, the answers to textbook problems, or reactions to music heard in a Music History class—you can keep up with what they publish. Some blogs also generate feeds for blog comments—be sure to add those, too, if you want to see all the feedback students receive through comment-enabled blogs. Our example, Movable Type, offers an Activity Feed that includes visitor feedback and activity reports for each blog. Movable Type (www.movabletype.com) also features blog tagging, and each can generate a custom tag-based feed. If students in your school are using one blog for different classes, they can "tag" their blog posts (English, math, art, etc.). You, the instructor, can simply subscribe to the group of posts that pertain to your class.

USING A WEB-BASED AGGREGATOR

There are a variety of free, Web-based news aggregators, including NewsGator Online (www.newsgator.com), My Yahoo! (http://my.yahoo.com), Google Reader (www.google.com/reader/), and Bloglines (www.bloglines.com). Visit one of these Web sites to check on your subscribed blogs instead of having to visit each one individually. As a bonus, many help you search for blogs, feeds, and information of interest such as the news or weather. All the online aggregators require an e-mail address to obtain an account. Because of this fact, it might not be the best solution for schools who do not issue student e-mail accounts. In this example, we will use Google Reader to subscribe an educator to both personal and professional sites. If you already are using Google Docs, you can use your same Google ID to access Reader.

First, let us start by looking at the Google Reader screen. I have already subscribed to a number of podcasts, blogs, and Web sites that all use either Atom or RSS to enable syndication. Navigation choices are listed on the left, and one of several views appears on the right, displaying the content from my feeds.

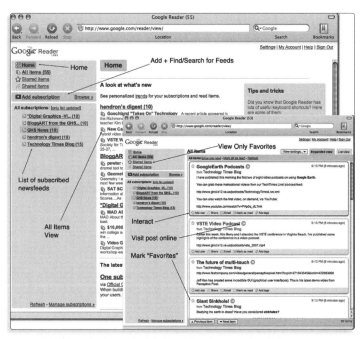

Figure 8.6 With navigation on the left, Google Reader puts subscription management on the side of the window, complete with a search function. A reader's search will automatically find the feed URLs for sites of interest. You can interact with feed items by marking them as favorites (star), e-mailing the content, and sharing content you find of interest.

There is one aspect of Google Reader I love, and that is how easy it is to share content. By clicking Share next to news posts that interest me, Google Reader sets up a custom Web page where colleagues or students can visit what I might find interesting or relevant, and it even generates a new RSS newsfeed. In the role of principal, I could ask my teachers to subscribe to this feed, automatically sending them articles of interest using Google Reader via Atom. As a teacher, I could pinpoint articles and blog posts of interest and then direct students to the Reader page where my shared items are collected. Finally, Google Reader can help you share your Shared Items through your blog. If you have access to change your blog's template, you can copy and paste JavaScript code from Google Reader and your blog will dynamically display new content that you share. Alternatively, Google's made it easy with a one-click button to add the shared items into your Blogger-hosted blog.

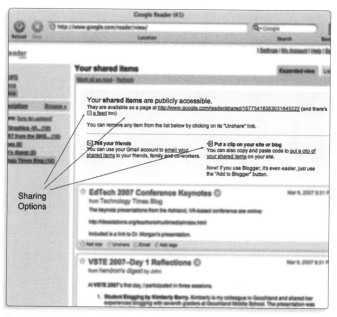

Figure 8.7 Within Google Reader, look for the methods in the yellow section, after clicking the Shared Items link on the top-left. You can share your content via e-mail or RSS.

From Google Reader's Home page, click the Add Subscription button on the left-hand side. Google Reader asks us for a newsfeed URL, or we can search for a feed. In this case, I want to add my superintendent's blog. (I already know it generates an RSS feed.) I type his name, plus the word "superintendent," with spaces in between each of the three words. I find quite a few sites that support RSS, and included in that collection is his blog's feed. Click on the Subscribe button beneath the match, and that's it!

Let us say I also want to keep up on developments in online assessment. Google Reader returns a number of popular Web sites—some are focused on online assessment, but others are more general and may or may not contain good content. So I typed "education online assessment," and then added the U.S. Department of Education, techLearning.com, and EdWeek.com to my subscribed feeds by clicking the "+Subscribe" button under each one.

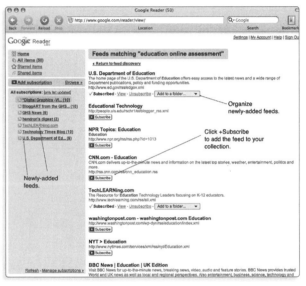

Figure 8.8 One of the found sites from a search entered in the green area, left (under Add Subscription), yielded a site without any feeds. The numbers after each feed represents the unread news items.

Because we all have interests outside of education, we can use Google Reader to subscribe to other Web-based content, too. The only problem is, we don't need to see our hobby-related content mixed together with professional content while at work. To rectify this, continue to paste-in feeds you already know, or utilize Google's search ability under Add Subscription to subscribe to more sites. Next, we will group the content into folders—the same way we did while using NetNewsWire.

Once you have found all of your feeds, click on Manage Subscriptions (lower-left of the window). With this screen, we can rename our feeds, remove them altogether, add tag words (e.g., "assessment," "science," "leadership," "Web 2.0," etc.) and tag feeds, or we can create and dump the feeds into folders. To create a new folder, start with your first feed, and click the Add to a Folder drop-down menu; then choose Create Folder. Once your folder names are created, use this pull-down menu to organize each feed. Your folder names will appear in the menu.

Figure 8.9 Once your feeds are organized into folders, you can then browse these bundled feeds together.

Web-based aggregators are a great way to organize content you regularly check online. For both subscribing and reading, each aggregator offers its own way of getting the job done. With an online aggregator, you cannot check feeds that are not on the Web (for instance, student blogs behind a firewall), but you also do not have to worry about leaving your computer on (and the aggregator running) to check your feeds throughout the day. The example we used here, Google Reader, makes it easy to organize your professional and personal feeds in one place. It also offers an innovative mechanism for sharing content of interest to you and others, through e-mail, a new Atom feed, or through a Web page.

USING AN EMBEDDED AGGREGATOR

Browsers will not be the last place we find embedded aggregators. They are already finding themselves on watches and in smart phones. Today, four major browsers—Internet Explorer 7, Safari, Firefox, and Opera—offer support for RSS. In this example, we will find newsfeeds of interest being published at our district and use Internet Explorer to subscribe to this content. As our last example illustrated, newsfeeds commonly accompany blogs, but they are also found as podcasts, news columns in Web sites, and in other customized lists and collections, such as Google Reader's shared feeds. In this example I will highlight some of the feeds used through the Web pages I manage for Goochland County Public Schools (www.glnd.k12.va.us).

I am interested in tracking several feeds associated with Goochland High School (www.glnd.k12.va.us/schools/ghs/). First, when

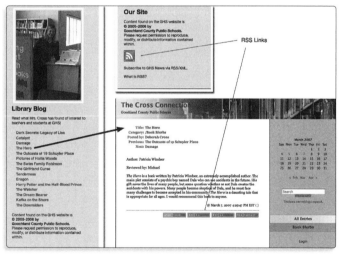

Figure 8.10 Look for RSS icons and the RSS badges for links to the RSS file. If you have the choice, as we do here, choose "RSS 2.0"—it is the more advanced of the newsfeed types. RSS is also behind the list of blog posts on the Library Blog snapshot, left. We take the RSS feed from the blog and process it so the links on the main library Web page appear dynamically. To find out how we did this, check out "RSS and Back Again" in appendix A.

I visit the high school's front page, I notice the now-familiar icon for RSS, as well as a link to Subscribe to GHS News. Next, I visit the high school media center's page and notice that the media specialist maintains a blog. While the most recent of the blog entries are listed on this page with links to each one, I would like to subscribe to everything she writes. Following one of the links takes me to her blog, where I find an RSS badge.

Going back to the high school site, I follow the link for Teachers and see that each one has a blog. I can follow a number of them, and in the same way I did for the media specialist's page, I click on the RSS links for each blog.

When I click on the RSS link at the high school's front page, Internet Explorer alerts me I have followed a link to a newsfeed. To confirm, I click on the Subscribe to This Feed button next to the favorites icon.

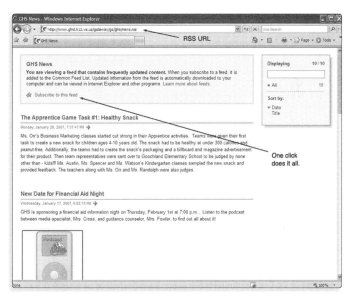

Figure 8.11 Internet Explorer refreshes the page when viewing a newsfeed. Click on the Subscribe link within the yellow box.

Because I am collecting a number of feeds from Goochland High School, after my first feed link, I create a new Goochland High School folder. I also have the option of re-naming the feed titles as I add them to my feeds collection.

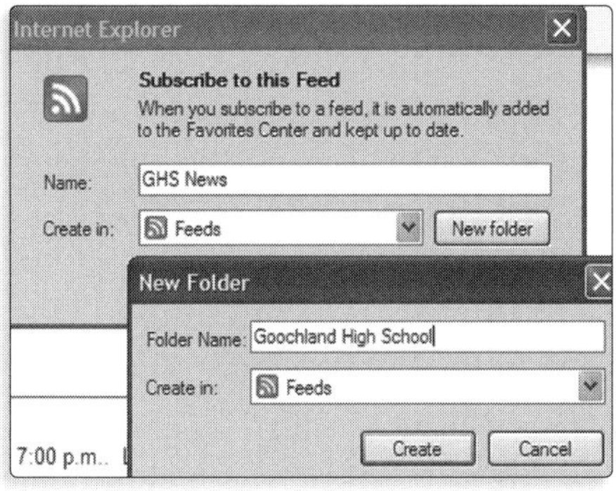

Figure 8.12 With Internet Explorer, you can create feed folders to organize your newsfeed content.

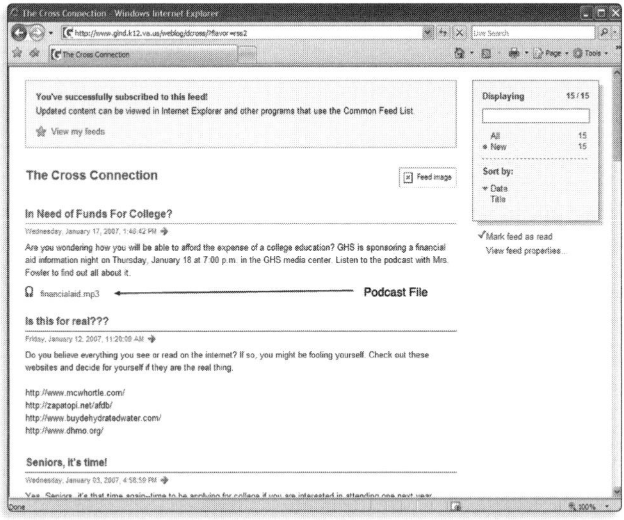

Figure 8.13 IE 7 confirms you have successfully added a feed. For our Goochland feeds, I had to change the URL header from "feed://" to "http://". IE displays podcasted content: it displays a *headphones* icon next to the embedded media files. If I had chosen the RSS 1.0 feed link, the multimedia content would not be included in the feed's display.

Once you have added a new feed to your collection, Internet Explorer displays a "You've successfully subscribed" message, and provides a link to visit your list of feeds. You can also use the Tools menu to show the feed list at any time.

Once I am done adding my feeds in IE, I visit the Favorites Center and take a look at my feeds. I have indeed captured what I set out to grab: GHS News, the Media Center blog, and three teacher blogs.

Figure 8.14
All the feeds in IE.

Each are nicely organized in the high school folder. Unlike with Net-NewsWire in our earlier example, clicking on the Goochland High School folder does not display all the high school feeds. Internet Explorer has not created true groups. Instead, I can click on each individual feed in the sidebar and read up on the new content.

Using a browser is a new and convenient way to keep track of Web content using RSS. The browsers do not yet offer all the functionality or flexibility of desktop and Web-based aggregators. All the browsers treat RSS feeds like individual pages and can be saved as "bookmarks" or "favorites" in the same way you keep Web site bookmarks. Now the browsers can "surf" on their own and simply let you know when your favorite pages are updated. For those of you who saw only gibberish when you clicked on RSS/XML links in the past, rest assured that the new class of browsers make better sense of syndicated content.

CHOOSING THE RIGHT AGGREGATOR

The three aggregator examples in this chapter (desktop-based, Web-based and browser-embedded) were chosen to demonstrate what is currently available when subscribing to newsfeeds. I highlighted some of the advantages and disadvantages of each. If you would like to use an aggregator with students (which, of course, I'm recommending), then choose something simple—the desktop- or browser-based scenario. If you have to track blogs that live behind a firewall (intranet versus Internet), then, again, a desktop- or browser-based aggregator is what you need. Desktop- and Web-based aggregators currently offer more features and convenience (e.g., tags and groups), and if you like to mix your podcast feeds and your blog feeds together, choose an aggregator that can handle both. Several of the options I have highlighted are free. And if you already use free Web services from Yahoo!, Google, or Ask.com, you might stay brand-loyal and use their solutions (My Yahoo!, Google Reader, and Bloglines). Bring on the newsfeeds!

PART 3

Classroom Applications

CHAPTER 9

Blogging with Students

ADDING TO A BODY OF COLLECTIVE KNOWLEDGE

Choice in today's society can be both a blessing and a curse. For example, if you live in a large city, deciding where to eat out with friends can be daunting: there are likely too many choices. The choices of content available on the Web—from research to enter-tainment—is mind-boggling. Reforms in schools for information literacy attempt to help students manage the expanding amount of content online. We all have favorite restaurants, but are you missing out on new choices by sticking to safe choices?

One method that has emerged online for helping each of us manage the plethora of Web sites and services is "tagging." Tagging is a method for assigning what librarians would call keywords to information we find. Tags are at the heart of two popular social Web sites, Flickr.com and del.icio.us. With Flickr, we can each upload photographs and tag them with our own keywords. If the photo I upload is of my dog, I might tag the photo "ralphie, dog, pets, virginia, summer, 2005." What makes Flickr's system of tagging social is that other Flickr users can use my tags, too. If you search for photos tagged "summer, 2005," "ralphie" will be somewhere in the results.

del.icio.us is a social bookmarking site. When I find a Web site of interest, I record its URL, its title, and my own set of tags. del.icio .us helps me by suggesting tags I have already used, and tags used by others to bookmark the site. I can later use del.icio.us to search for sites others have tagged. If I am having trouble finding a good site for troubleshooting the installation of software, I might use del .icio.us to search for "troubleshoot vista install." Blogs, too, are now supporting tagging conventions used elsewhere. Blog search engines such as Technorati (www.technorati.com) use blogger-added tags to help improve their search results.

With so much content already online, and new schemes emerging to help find it all, you might ask why we should ask our students to add to what content already exists? What benefits can student bloggers expect? For one, many students are participating already in the "blogosphere" through social Web sites such as Bebo (www. bebo.com), Facebook (www.facebook.com), and MySpace (www. myspace.com). I believe we are obligated to educate students on how to responsibly and safely manage online communities where blogging, or practices much like it, thrive.

Beyond lessons in Internet safety and information literacy, something much more compelling can come from using blogs in schools. Alan November, a popular speaker and education consultant, has asked: "Are we simply preparing kids to go into the business world by getting them to understand technology? Or are we trying to transform the culture of teaching and learning to really prepare kids to be self-motivated, true lifelong learners?" (McClosky, 2006). The Read/Write Web can transform learning and teaching culture, and November (www.novemberlearning.com), along with former teacher Will Richardson (www.weblogg-ed.com), believe tools such as blogs can turn what we traditionally consider an information source into a learning environment. In short, blogs are, together and separately, introspective, public, challenging, engaging, social, and connected entities that students create. Blogs can be an ultimate form of evidence of what students are learning. Blogs not only become digital portfolios for student work but also digital notebooks that capture facts and emotional memories. Blogs enable students to link to other sources of content, including other blogs. Through blogs, students can build their own version of content that can accompany their learning for as long as the blog remains online.

SET CLEAR GOALS

Before embarking into the blogosphere with students, carefully consider what the exercise of blogging will accomplish. Is this something students will want to keep for the duration of a course, or for the duration of their career in a particular school? Will the blog be something they keep for life? Once we settle on the planned lifespan of the blog, consider the audience. Is the blog being maintained primarily for the instructor? For the student? For the student's peers? If the blog is public, you may encourage students to use a handle instead of their real name, thereby enabling them to be honest—to share personal experiences and to ultimately encourage authenticity in their writing, all the while maintaining their privacy and/or anonymity.

Will the blog be only for class work, or can students add their own reflections? Can students create blog posts for personal issues? Will you encourage other students to post comments and responses to their peers' blogs?

The goals you set for inviting students to blog within a school course or project need to drive the answers to these and other questions. The answers may help direct some choices you have when choosing where and when to blog. If you invite students to blog about personal issues, do they have the capability to screen (or filter) who can read each post? As stated elsewhere in this book, review and update your school's Acceptable Use Policy (AUP) before blogging with students. The Electronic Frontier Foundation has published items to consider (www.eff.org/bloggers/lg/faq-students.php) for the rights of student bloggers. Many educators believe that blogs can be a powerful communications tool. The goals for using blogs in the classroom should capture the unique benefits that the Read/Write Web offers all school stakeholders.

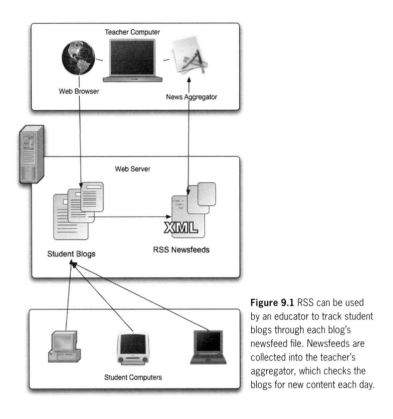

Figure 9.1 RSS can be used by an educator to track student blogs through each blog's newsfeed file. Newsfeeds are collected into the teacher's aggregator, which checks the blogs for new content each day.

**BLOGGING IN THE CLASSROOM:
BLOGS FOR PRODUCTIVITY IN LEARNING**

◆ **Example 1:** *Hunter's Closure*

Content area: All subject areas

Synopsis: This blogging technique takes Madeline Hunter's lesson component Closure into the modern age by asking students to reflect upon a lesson's content through the blog. Did your students really "get it" in today's lesson? Read their blogs to find out. This outline can be used as a portion of any number of lessons where access to Internet-connected computers is at hand.

Standards: NETS•S: 2.b; 5.a, c; 6.b

Age: Grades 7–12

Objectives: For the reinforcement of learning objectives, students use the blog to organize their learning through reflection.

Resources: computer, blog

Procedure: Closure should happen in a lesson each time an important milestone in learning occurs. Many times this is at the end of each lesson unit. Students are asked to author a new blog post, prompted by various questions and instructions, including:

1. What confused me about today's lesson?

2. Summarize the main points of today's activity.

3. What new stuff did you learn today?

4. Write the most important aspect of what you learned today.

5. Based on what you learned, what else do you need to review before you feel you understand it completely?

Assessment: Closure can be a summarization activity for students. Closure is also an informal assessment tool. What do students know and not know after today's learning experience? The blogs here are learning journals that help the educator plan the next lesson. Because blogs among the class can be read, learners returning to other students' blog posts for the next lesson can provide the teacher a hook for the start of a new lesson.

Notes: If you follow the tenets of Madeline Hunter's Instructional Theory into Practice, you know how important closure is in a lesson involving direct instruction. When both the teacher and the students have ready access to authoring blog posts, students can use the blog as the technology to journal the close of each lesson. This works well in one-to-one environments and for when classes are taught in the computer lab.

With modern demands for accountability, knowing how successful each lesson affected learning is paramount information for each teacher. While paper notebooks can be used in lieu of a blog, the electronic blog itself offers the social, collaborative edge. One lesson's closure is another lesson's anticipatory set. With a blog, students not only have access to what they learned, but what their peers learned as well. The act of self-reflection, encouraged through the reading of other student blog posts, reinforces Hunter's concept of a well-planned lesson.

◆ Example 2: *Marzano's Notebook*

Content area: All subject areas

Synopsis: Students use blogs as digital notebooks in practice of Robert Marzano's techniques in the book *Classroom Instruction That Works* (Marzano, Pickering, & Pollock, 2004). Specifically, blogs can be used by students to incorporate Marzano's Identifying Similarities and Differences, Summarizing, and Cooperative Learning techniques. Portions of this example can be used in a variety of lessons where access to Internet-based computers is available.

Standards: NETS•S: 1.a, b, d; 2.b, d; 3.b; 4.c; 5.a; 6.b

Age: Grades 5–12

Objectives: Students will use blogs as the center of a digital notebook to continuously record input from a variety of learning experiences, including the analysis of facts and concepts, the summarization of text, spoken word, and video presentations. Students will compare their blogs to other classmates' when researching solutions to problems presented in solitary and collaborative investigations.

Resources: Textbooks, Web resources, blogs, computer, rubrics (http://pblchecklist.4teachers.org/checklist.shtml). This lesson is facilitated with a one-to-one computer initiative, or regular access to a networked-based computer.

Procedure:

1. In the student-centered, project-based classroom, students are their own best resources for creating new knowledge. For a variety of subject areas, the blog becomes the "dumping ground" for knowledge.

2. Students maintain blog categories for each subject area (e.g., science, mathematics, English, etc.).

3. Students create blog posts and record the similarities and differences between different concepts.

4. Students create blog posts to record summaries of written texts, spoken-word presentations, and video clips.

5. Students read and comment on peer blog posts to support conclusions in project-based activities.

Assessment: Do students accurately summarize content, identify similarities and differences, and work in virtual groups to solve problems? The learning project may be assessed through rubrics.

Notes: You may ask, "If Marzano's research-backed techniques already work well, what is gained by using a blog?" For one, blogs enable groups of students to access and assess one another's *notes*—their observations, reflections, and summarization of content. Two, blogs can facilitate project-based learning by filtering and organizing a student's own interaction with basic content, setting the stage for higher-order thinking skills. How will students answer a complex question? They need to consider different points of view, make connections between different content areas, and synthesize information. The blog as the ultimate notebook enables students to cross-link blog posts across different explorations of course content using proven methods. In the context of a PBL (project-based learning) lesson, students tap into their own collective knowledge, as published in the blog, to reach a solution to an essential question through carefully planned activities. The blog can also assist the instructor in monitoring the projects that students tackle alone and in groups.

The philosophy behind project-based learning focuses on students creating new knowledge from a lesson that centers around an essential question. Students need preparation for answering such a question. Here, the blog is used as a scaffolding device. I call this "Marzano's" notebook because the blog is used here to encourage three of his classroom practices to refocus the classroom in order to support a student-centered approach. Blogs used this way will work best in a school where cooperative learning is already taking place between teachers of disparate subject areas. While this can be used within a project-based unit, it also works with direct-instruction models and in units of study, both short and extended.

BLOGGING IN THE CLASSROOM: BLOGGING LESSONS

◆ Lesson 1: *Blogging the Maya*

Content area: Social studies

Synopsis: This lesson makes use of the "Marzano's Notebook," example lesson.

Students will use blogs to summarize a collection of video clips focused on the ancient Mayan civilization in Mesoamerica. Students will next be grouped to analyze the summaries that members of the group created individually, and then examine the similarities and differences between their summaries. Students will develop questions that they will post to their blogs, highlighting the differences they found, along with yet-unanswered questions of interest about Mayan civilization. Students next post to their blogs a script used to develop their own informative video about Mayan civilization. Before the video project is attempted, other students in the class comment on their blogged-script with constructive criticism. Students construct a short video presentation on Mayan culture using digital photographs or images captured from the video segments.

The blog in this lesson facilitates cooperative learning between different groups: partners and whole-class interaction. As the instructor monitors student summaries, students may be asked to re-watch clips for inaccuracies and/or refinement ideas.

What is interesting is that even when two people listen to the same presentation, the recall of what was important or salient will vary between individuals. Students gain the practice here of comparing various accounts in order to arrive at a consensus: what was similar between one summary and the next? This may be used to set up future learning where students interview witnesses to an event: did every witness hear and see the same thing?

Standards: NCSS: I, III
NETS•S: 1.a, b, d; 2.b, d; 3.b; 4.c; 5.a; 6.b

Age: Grades 6–8

Objectives: Students will learn about Mayan culture through watching video clips and creating their own video presentation. Students will use blogs to collect information, develop a script, and solicit feedback for the video presentation from classmates and the instructor.

Resources: Video presentations on Mayan civilization (services such as Discovery Education *unitedstreaming* and Safari Montage offer short video clips in an online, digital format), blogs, digital story-telling software (Apple iMovie, Microsoft Photo Story), online and traditional resources on Mayan civilization at the students' reading level.

Procedure:

1. Students will be introduced to the blog and the instructions for this project.

2. Students will watch a series of short video clips, being asked to give the clips their full attention—for trying to recognize and remember what is important in each video.

3. Students independently summarize the content of each video clip into a blog post. Each blog post title identifies the video clip's title.

4. Students are paired with a partner in front of the computer, and they compare what's the same and different between their summarizations. These are marked on a worksheet, and the differences between summaries are transferred to a new blog post on each blog.

5. Student partners decide if there is more they would like to learn about Mayan/Mesoamerican culture, and they add these augmentations to the second blog post on summarization differences.

6. Students use secondary sources provided by the instructor (e.g., books and Web resources) to research the "truth" behind different summarizations, and to search for answers to their questions.

7. Students use supplied digital photos and stills from the video clips to plan a storyboard that presents the most important information about Mayan culture.

8. Students write their video-project script and post it to their blogs.

9. The instructor reviews the student scripts with critiques. The instructor may invite other students to comment on scripts as well.

10. Following a model for digital storytelling, students develop a slideshow of photos and record their video script.

11. Students share the video project presentations on Mayan culture with their classroom peers.

Assessment: Students will be aided by a timeline for the completion of each step in this project. A rubric assessment will be used:

1. For this project, were good-quality contributions made regularly and on time to the blog?

2. Did your summaries capture the details presented in the videos about Mayan culture?

3. Did you and your partner pose more questions about the life and history of the Mayan civilization?

4. Did you and your partner find answers to your questions?

5. Did you complete a storyboard for the planning of your video project, marked with photos, graphics and video?

6. Does the video play back smoothly?

7. Did you and your partner equally share the responsibility for recording and editing your video project?

8. Does the video present some of the facts generated by your research and video-clip summaries?

9. Is there evidence in your final video project of critiques/improvements raised by your instructor and classmates?

Notes: The student video projects may be turned into podcasts and published on an internal Web site or within a closed course management system. The lesson idea used here can obviously be used with any historical topic. While summarization and comparing similarities and differences are two Marzano techniques used here, the real emphasis is collaboration in small and large groups. Students will use blogs here as a productivity tool, to collect their work together with the larger class corpus. Each major step in the project may be divided to span across the entire school year. The student videos may be shown at the end of the year, for instance, as a capstone review.

The one weakness in this lesson is the enforcement of learning standards for the topic studied. Will students cover all the salient, important facets of ancient Mayan civilization as prescribed by your local standards? Will they ask the right questions to fill in the gaps? Success in meeting standards requirements for this lesson will rely upon carefully chosen clips, instructor coaching, and instructor comments on blog posts created throughout the project.

The summarization of video clips will likely work best with shorter clips (less than 90 seconds), depending on the age level. This encourages the use of more clips. The instructor can facilitate the distribution of clips if they use digital video clips, which can be posted in their own blog. Older students may also consult primary sources, such as a translation of Mayan scripture from the *Popol Vuh*.

If teachers' blogs are used to post video clips, or if student blogs are used to post video projects using copyright-protected content, ensure that the blogs are either *protected* with a password (as part of an intranet-based network) or closed within a course management system.

● Lesson 2: *Keeping a Fine Arts Portfolio*

Content area: Visual arts, music

Synopsis: Students will use the potential audience offered through the Web to publish original works and develop an electronic (or "digital") portfolio through a blog. The blog medium allows visitors to the blog site to comment on the student work. In this lesson, the instructor makes it a requirement (for each artifact published) for students to solicit a comment from a friend, family member, or other educator.

Standards: NA-M.9–12.6, 7
NA-VA.9–12.5
NETS•S: 1.a, b; 2.a, b; 3.b; 5.a, d; 6.b

Age: Grades 6–12+

Objectives: By creating a digital portfolio, students will see their creative works through the eyes and ears of an authentic audience. Students will use comments made by visitors to their blog to re-work and re-examine their creative process. Students will be evaluated on finding at least one different artifact evaluator for each posting, and using text within the blog to describe their creative work and the media used in their work.

Resources: Blog account with support for images and/or sound files and comments. Students will need access to auxiliary equipment for posting their work online, possibly including scanners, digital cameras, photo editing software (Adobe Photoshop, Photoshop Elements, or GIMP [GNU Image Manipulation Program]), microphones, and audio mastering software (Audacity). This project may benefit from voice comments made by visitors to the portfolio using a service called Vaestro (www.vaestro.com).

Procedure:

1. Through an art or music class, students will work through several creative projects throughout the course. Each time a work is completed, it is digitized and uploaded to a blog, complete with a description about the work and the media used to create it.

2. Other classmates, a chosen reviewer, and the public at large will have the opportunity to view the class-created portfolios and submit comments.

3. Students may respond to comments and questions to clarify others' understanding of their work.

4. Students will have the option and time to revise their creative work, and to re-post the result through the blog.

5. The instructor evaluates student participation in creating and reviewing portfolios, and may also judge the portfolio based on aesthetic criteria or the development of skills throughout the course.

Assessment: Teachers may design a rubric that supports the lesson procedures and objectives.

Notes: This lesson may be adapted to include other assignments outside the subject areas of music and fine arts. For advanced students, the lesson can accommodate the student-creation of a blog template for the look and design of the blog Web site. Many bloggers would label these sites as "audioblogs" or "photoblogs." Students might be encouraged to continue their digital portfolio beyond the course (e.g., during the summer). Also, consider the value of what students are potentially publishing online. Since students own the copyright of their creative works, your school may ask students or their parents to sign a copyright waiver, thereby granting the school permission to publish their works online. The blog portfolios should include a copyright message that warns visitors not to distribute or reproduce student works.

For a smaller-scale implementation, students may be invited to a community/group blog by the instructor (each with rights to make posts), where an entire class' work is on display.

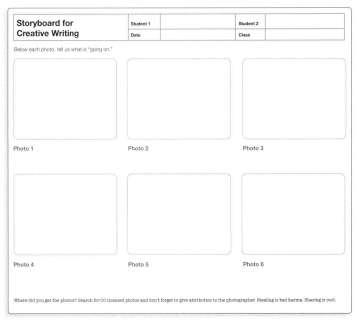

Figure 9.2 Encourage students to use a storyboard like this to help them organize their concept before blogging. This can be re-created in a word processor application so that digital photos can be dropped into each frame.

◆ Lesson 3: *Blogs for Creative Writing*

Content area: English, writing

Synopsis: Students will use blogs to support creative writing. Student writing through blogs will encourage story development and will use visual prompts to generate story ideas.

Standards: NCTE: 4, 5, 8, 9, 11, 12
          NETS•S: 1.a, b; 2.a, b; 5.a

Age: Grades 8–12

Objectives: Students will use visual imagery to focus elements of a creative story and write with a partner through a group blog. Partner groups will be assessed on their allegiance to the pictures in the development of their story and on the coherency between their collaborative efforts. Reflections from other class members will provide critique of the creative story through blog comments.

Resources: digital photographs, group blog, storyboard worksheet

Procedure:
1. Students will be grouped into partners and presented with a series of digital images.

2. Students will be asked to brainstorm ideas about what is taking place in each picture.

3. Students will organize the digital pictures into a sequence to be used for a creative-writing story. The student pairs will complete a storyboard worksheet, complete with a sequence of pictures and short descriptions that will become key elements in the story.

4. Students alternate writing the short story in a blog. Every other post is written by the other student in the pair. While each student is following the same basic plan (outlined by the storyboard), each student has the opportunity to add creative twists and present challenges to their co-writer.

5. Students may include the digital pictures to help illustrate the story.

6. After a number of exchanges, the stories are read by classmates in blog-post chronological order, and critiques are posted to the blogs as comments.

Assessment: Students are exploring story development and unexpected twists in a story. They are constrained by the collection of digital photographs available. Students will be assessed individually in a rubric based on the following criteria:

1. Does the story capture the action and setting presented in the digital photographs?

2. Do both students equally contribute content through the blog?

3. Does a pre-writing storyboard represent major events in the story's timeline?

4. Did the individuals creatively respond to one another's independent writing?

5. Did the story as a whole show unity?

6. Did the team contribute positive comments to other writers through blog comments?

Notes: This lesson may be challenging for some students. This lesson is essentially an exercise for students to communicate and to synthesize different creative ideas into something unified. Community blogs are blogs that are authored by more than one person. In this case, two students contribute to one blog. Other Read/Write tools could be used here, from a Web-based word processor (Google Docs) to a wiki. The blog format includes the ability to add comments, and stories can easily be followed through RSS newsfeeds.

Some teachers may choose to use blogs—writing that is quick and spontaneous—as a first-draft version of creative stories. The lesson may be repeated using items other than photos to begin the organizational/planning stages of writing. Try musical clips, scenes from movies and television, or physical items found around the house.

Lesson 4: *Let's Review*

Content area: English, journalism, media studies

Synopsis: Students follow journalism ethics in authoring reviews of creative media, including motion pictures, books, and musical recordings.

Standards: Society of Professional Journalists Ethics
           NCTE: 2, 4, 7, 8, 12
           NETS•S: 1.a, b; 2.b; 3.c; 4.c, d; 6.a

Age: Grades 9–12

Objectives: Students apply the journalist's ethical standards in the writing of a critical review of a motion picture, book, or musical recording, citing both positive and negative aspects of the work. Students write with a clear voice, supporting their opinion of the creative work with comments on the work's structure, a comparison of similar or dissimilar works, and by quoting the opinions of noted experts or scholars.

Resources: computer, blog, media for review

Procedure:

1. With the instructor's approval, students choose to review a movie, book, or musical recording.

2. Students review the Society of Professional Journalists' ethics guidelines (www.spj.org/ethicscode.asp).

3. Students author a review of their creative-media choice and publish it as a blog post.

4. Student peers read the reviews and answer assessment questions in the blog comments.

5. Ideally, each review will be read by five students. Each "yes" response to the following assessment questions yields one point. Student reviews are therefore awarded 0–25 points total.

Assessment: Student writings will be critiqued by their peers through blog comments, which will ask readers the following questions:

1. Can I tell if you like or dislike this work?

2. Do you cite something positive about this work?

3. Does the review make comment on the work's structure (the formula used to build the movie, book, or music)?

4. Are quotes or references to other opinions accurate?

5. Is the work compared to the qualities of other (competing) works?

Notes: Being a critic is not easy. A critic must use critical-thinking skills to weigh both the good and the bad, and to *support* his or her positive and/or unfavorable arguments. By publishing their reviews online through a blog, students are adding to the growing amount of independent criticism from the blogosphere. This lesson can be expanded by including Web-based research for other reviews, including those found on community-based Web sites such as Amazon.com. Students may respond to other reviews, creating a persuasive essay on why they find the review strong or weak. This lesson attempts to encourage integrity by introducing students to critical-thinking skills and professional standards of ethics when writing. Following ethical guidelines grants the students' reviews authority in a sea of free-floating opinions.

Lesson 5: *Let's Collaborate: Viewpoints on Current Events*

Content area: World languages, social studies

Synopsis: The classic lesson of pairing students who are learning a foreign language with pen pals here pairs students together with blogs. Students are paired with students from a different culture, and together they use one another's language to address common problems facing society (e.g., global warming, humanitarianism, economic development, and politics). Students can communicate through one shared blog or through individual blogs and blog comments.

Standards: NSFLE: 1.1, 1.2, 1.3, 2.1, 2.2, 3.1, 3.2, 4.1
NCSS: I, II, IV, V, IX
NETS•S: 1.b; 2.a, b, c; 3.d; 4.a; 5.b; 6.a

Age: Grades 11–12

Objectives: Students will use Web resources to identify problems and issues in their country that have a global impact. Students will consider solutions to these issues and the solution's impact on individuals with different cultural beliefs in other parts of the world. Students will consider their solutions and ideas by writing through blogs in a foreign language with other students who are native speakers of the language being studied. Students will be assessed by the frequency and accuracy of their communication and by their ability to manage a collaborative relationship with their blogging counterpart.

Resources: news Web sites (news.yahoo.com, news.google.com, etc.), blogs.

Procedure:

1. The instructor will arrange the lesson with another teacher. (For sites where teachers can begin collaborative projects, see appendix A, Web Resources for RSS, Podcasting, and Social Computing).

2. Students will research the Web for current events and issues in their own countries that carry global impact. Global warming, politics, immigration, economic development, humanitarian projects, and so forth, can all be possible areas of interest.

3. Students begin their blog by writing in the native language of their counterpart, introducing a respective issue and why it impacts people in their country and beyond.

4. Counterpart students do the same on their blog. The instructor may set up a single blog for both students or a class blog to share. Blogs can be managed with multiple bloggers and content using tags or blog categories.

5. Students continue to regularly blog, proposing solutions to the issue that has been selected.

6. Next, students respond to one another's solutions through blog comments.

7. Other students in the class are invited to read through the partner exchange and give their own take on the proposed solutions.

8. Students complete an inventory once the exchange is complete, focusing on:

   a. What was learned about the other student's culture?

   b. Were the solutions proposed viable?

   c. How difficult was it to get your own points across?

   d. Did you see eye to eye, or not?

   e. What did your exchange with another student teach you about yourself?

Assessment: A rubric assessment is used to assess students in the project.

1. Was the appropriate vocabulary used in your online discussions?

2. Did you use correct grammar, spelling, and punctuation?

3. Did you choose a topic of interest not only to the people in your country, but to people elsewhere?

4. Did you regularly contribute to the discussion and pose reasonable solutions?

5. Did you complete the self-evaluation inventory?

Notes: Communicating with people from different cultures can be difficult, the language barrier notwithstanding. This lesson is ultimately one centered around being an effective communicator. While the lesson is primarily focused on pairing students together and communicating in each other's native language, the public nature of blogs enables the instructor to invigorate the discussion by including other students with different cultural perspectives. Written communication skills are the focus here, but also an awareness of issues facing the world.

The blogging discussion's focus on current issues can obviously be changed. Other topics could explore the ethics behind scientific research, the importance of various historical figures, and the aspects of each student's daily life. Students should be encouraged to back up any cultural assertions they make with related Web sources and links of interest.

CONCLUSION

To blog is to write. With the number of blogs now approaching 100 million by some accounts (since the online genre emerged in the late 1990s), it's clear they're here to stay. The future acquisition of information for today's students may in fact rest on the content created every minute through the blogosphere. Through blogging, students will come to realize that all information found in blogs must be scrutinized. Through educational channels, students will find blogs as mechanisms for connecting with colleagues and friends, for linking to other online information sources, and for simply reflecting on life. Blogs can be a starting point for both solving problems and for finding a creative outlet.

As educators integrate the use of blogs in the technology-infused classroom, they will find, in addition, blogs can support learning productivity, from reinforcing lesson closure, to encouraging students to summarize the content they read and take notes on what they learn.

CHAPTER 10

Wikis for the Classroom

As I noted previously, wikis are primarily a convenience, a productivity tool for the Web. Unlike RSS-enabled calendars, social Web sites, or the comments and trackbacks of blogs, wikis are not particularly fancy. In essence, wiki documents are linked pages. As we also examined in the earlier chapters, wiki engines offer a variety of control for who creates, reads, and changes content.

Is it the creation, sharing, and access to content that make wikis a powerful classroom tool? It may ultimately be just a convenient productivity tool, but there is nothing inconsequential about convenience and time saved in the classroom, or about a wiki's ability to foster collaboration, review, and revision among students.

Before embarking on the use of a wiki in the classroom, decisions should be made regarding who will host the content (your school, the district, or a third-party provider), what wiki software you will use, and whether you'll need support for attachments and content beyond text. In Part 1 of this book we examined wikis and mentioned some free online solutions. PBwiki (http://pbwiki.com) and Wikispaces (www.wikispaces.com) are two services that will carry the burden of hosting content, and the price is right. If you are choosing a solution to host on your server (with more security and the ability to close the wiki behind your firewall), I recommend PmWiki and Instiki. PmWiki offers more features (file attachments and control of access to wiki areas by groups), but it works best on a standalone server. Instiki offers fewer features but can easily run on the teacher's own laptop. The example lessons that follow can use either of these choices. For the first and most ambitious example, I recommend using MediaWiki (www.mediawiki.org/wiki/MediaWiki/), the wiki engine that powers Wikipedia (http://wikipedia.org). I recommend you get tech support for the installation of MediaWiki. Once it is set up, it is easy to use.

WIKI EXAMPLE 1: THE SCHOOL KNOWLEDGE BASE

This project can be a small one, or it can expand to be a giant undertaking. The idea behind it, however, is simple: students in a class or a school build their own version of a wikipedia (a wiki-based encyclopedia) using the same software that powers Wikipedia. If we consider this project as a school-wide endeavor, everyone must buy-in to the project and its merits. What it does—and why you should consider it—is this: it puts students in charge of creating their own digital encyclopedia. Think of it as a knowledge base supported through teacher and peer review. The content can be as simple as dictionary entries for vocabulary words to more profound examples, including entries that combine factual content alongside personal commentary. A school-created knowledge base can include school rules contributed by administration, resources for every content standard created by students, copious links to resources on the Web that support each entry or article, and classroom expectations and syllabi contributed by teachers.

What might be the lessons learned? Students learn about media and information literacy: anyone can publish content, and it does not matter how professional or "pretty" it looks. Students will learn that opinions (under the scrutiny of peers) have different value than factual information. By asking a student body to maintain their own knowledge base, we as educators approach the ultimate lesson in the evaluation of sources.

How the Wiki Knowledge Base Works

1. The school establishes a wiki server. This is a Web server that lives "out" on the Internet or "inside" a school's network. A dedicated personal computer that can be regularly backed-up will work. I recommend the wiki software MediaWiki. Each student can be given a unique login, and logins can be required to change content.

2. Guidelines are established for the wiki-powered knowledge base. First, everyone can contribute. Second, use of the knowledge base must fit within the realm of your school's or district's Acceptable Use Policy (AUP), which likely states that the site cannot be used for profit, advertisement, or the intimidation of others. Third, teachers, technology personnel, and administrators must all pitch in to manage the wiki server. Teachers should be held responsible for what their students post online. Fourth, the knowledge base should support cooperative, collaborative learning, which wikis do by nature. Lastly, the knowledge base should be used not just as a place to post student content, but as an authoritive reference tool. Class assignments, quizzes, and other learning endeavors should encourage the use of the knowledge base.

3. Teachers should assign individual students and student groups the responsibility of building individual articles.

4. All articles should integrate the use of rich media, when available. This includes photos, illustrations, movies, and audio clips. One group of students may be responsible for the text while another could be in charge of the rich media.

5. Students and school faculty should all play an active role in assessing the quality of the articles. The Discussion tab within MediaWiki's interface, or a notes section, can be used by educators to make suggestions, comments, or critiques to the content.

Educators who have already engaged their students with Read/Write opportunities of expression know how their students are powerfully motivated by being able to publish their work online for others to see, hear, and use. On a much larger level, this is how Wikipedia works. It may generate concerns from many perspectives, but the concept behind it—free access, community contributions, refinements for accuracy, and errors in a malleable state—survives and even thrives.

What would it take for such a project to work? It is ambitious, but not impossible. Students would require only ready access to a computer to effectively use the wiki knowledge base as a resource, learning tool, and a commons to "hang" what they are learning about in the classroom. This project could thrive in a one-to-one environment, but also could work in a classroom with a number of reliable personal computers.

Organizing a Knowledge Base Wiki

How might a project like a school-based wiki be managed? Would the goal be to build it in one year? Or would the wiki live beyond the school year, getting richer and fuller and growing each month? The folks behind Wikipedia see their project as a continually evolving one, but one that also will have "snapshot versions." At some point, they plan to freeze the Wikipedia, slap a version number on it, and disable editing options for that version. I think that solution could very well work in a school setting. I would recommend a three-to-four-year period. After all, the project should reflect the efforts of those students who are actively using it.

Classroom Uses of the Wiki Knowledge Base

1. Create a wiki page for your list of content standards. For a study guide, link to all the articles that support those standards.

2. Create articles for spelling and vocabulary. For more sophistication, include audio clips for pronunciation.

3. Create articles for math algorithms—formulaic methods for solving arithmetic and word problems.

4. Assign groups to create articles for major works of literature, music, and art.

5. Create articles for each sport played in physical education classes. Include video clips of the sports being played.

6. Create articles for scientific investigations. Concurrent classes can compare their results to similar experiments, or expand upon the earlier research of others.

7. Create articles for events in history, including public-domain visuals and movie clips.

8. Create timelines. The events in timelines can link to individual articles covering the topics in more depth.

9. Create summary articles. Since the knowledge base is *school* based, link to articles demonstrating prior knowledge.

10. Scrutinize, review, and refine. Assign the task of maintaining a wiki to include peer review.

FINAL THOUGHTS

I have not yet seen this project take place in a school, but I am anxious to see it attempted. Such a project takes the vision and support of a large group of people. Building a school-based wiki is firmly rooted in a social-constructivist, student-centered, teacher-as-coach-style educational approach. The tools of learning are student-created. This idea is similar to the idea of students building their own "learning database" in a blog. Unlike with the informality of a blog, a wiki project involves every learner with access to a Web browser, thus raising the bar for the expectations of both quantity and quality. We are part of a new society; one actively collaborating through social technologies, which may be the future of our global economy. It follows that maintaining a school-based knowledge base would make for an incredible learning experience.

In the lessons that follow, we focus on simpler, smaller-scale uses for wikis in the classroom.

◆ Lesson 1: *Personal Logs*

Content area: Health, family and consumer science

Synopsis: Students use a wiki to record personal data relating to nutrition and fitness over a period of time. Each student uses their own wiki page to report and record data, including the amount of exercise they perform each day and the number of calories consumed. Students can study a variety of health factors, including mood, body temperature, weight, amount of sleep, and body mass to draw conclusions about how exercise and food choices make them feel.

Standards: NHES: 1.8.1, 1.12.1, 1.8.2, 1.12.2
NETS•S: 1.d; 3.b, d; 4.c

Age: Grades 6–12

Objectives: Students will study the impact of personal choices on their health by collecting data about their sleep patterns, diet, and exercise. Students will collect their data and post it to a wiki server. Students will compare their data to national standards and class standards, and draw conclusions about the impact their choices have on their own feelings of well-being.

Resources: wiki access; scale; skinfold calipers for measuring body mass index (BMI); thermometer; articles detailing healthy lifestyle choices; record keeping for sleep, meals, and snacks

Procedure:

1. Students will each read an article outlining healthy lifestyle choices. They will summarize their article at the top of their wiki page. Students will unknowingly be assigned different articles.

2. Students will begin recording various data on their wiki pages. The wiki pages should remain private for each student. The data may include weight, BMI, amount of daily sleep, calories consumed at each meal, number of carbohydrates eaten at each meal, descriptions of mood and state of mind, body temperature, and exercise (including type and duration of exercise). Data should be collected and recorded each day.

3. After a short period of time, students will compare their lifestyle choices with those suggested in the article. Students will write on the wiki a reflection of their record keeping. What surprised them? Do they feel the suggestions made in the article are realistic?

4. In a class discussion, students will share what their different articles suggested. Students will compare and contrast the suggestions made (e.g., What behaviors

seem to be common themes between articles? How different do some articles differ in their suggestions for diet and exercise?).

5. Students continue their record keeping for one month.

6. Students draw conclusions from their data-collection research. Based on their research, they will answer the following questions, with quantitative examples from their data set:

   a. Did my amount of sleep affect my mood?

   b. Did the amount of calories affect the amount of time I spent exercising?

   c. How consistent was my body temperature? Did it coincide with mood swings?

   d. Did the amount of sleep affect the time I spent exercising?

   e. Did recording my weight change my attitude about what I ate?

   f. Did my BMI change over the month? Why might it have changed (or remained constant)?

   g. Based on the articles the class read and on what I eat, how much I exercise, and the amount of time I spend sleeping, am I leading a healthy lifestyle?

7. Students select data they would like to share among the class. Examples might include amounts of sleep, BMI, or calories consumed. Students will indicate on their wiki page how their numbers compared with the class average.

8. The instructor will seek out sources of national data for the types of observations students make. Students will compare the national data with their own.

9. Considering the articles, analysis of data between individuals, the respective class, and a national or state comparison, students are asked to draw conclusions about what they have learned with questions such as these:

   a. How important is exercise as a contribution toward a healthy lifestyle?

   b. How is your sense of well-being affected by diet and exercise?

   c. What else could we have measured that has an impact on health?

   d. Were you surprised by what you learned about your class?

   e. If you had a friend who was engaging in unhealthy lifestyle choices, how might you encourage them to change? And by how much?

Assessment: Students will be assessed by the quantity and quality of data they collected, by participation in requested responses, and by the quality of those responses. The responses should be supported with data or expert opinions. The ultimate objective is to examine exercise and eating habits (and the difficulty in changing those habits for the better) in order to inspire an attitude change for students who are making unhealthy lifestyle choices.

Notes: The wiki in this case is a productivity tool that offers students a secure area to post their data, which in turn enables the instructor to assess their data. The instructor may choose to collect only a subset of the data suggested here and make the wiki pages public to the class. Using data, responses, and reflections, wiki pages can foster online communication through the establishment of different wiki pages.

The data collected in this lesson can also be maintained on a desktop or an online spreadsheet, such as that found at Google Docs. The lesson can be expanded to include aspects of the scientific method, including drawing conclusions, graphing skills, and analyzing mathematical data. The data collected might also include student notes about *why* choices were made. Why, for example, did a student choose an unhealthy snack over a healthy snack? Was it peer pressure? A bad or carefree mood? Marketing and advertising? The lesson here is centered on health and wellness, but it could easily expand to business and marketing.

While the wiki is a great organizational and productivity tool for logging thoughts, data, and responses in a semi-public space, the real benefit of the tool is apparent when students are asked to discuss, compare, and analyze their collective data. The wiki can capture all of this digitally, thus creating a database that can empower students with the objective of the lesson—being able to see both the macro and micro picture of their choices within the class and in their own lives. Digital data, including student thoughts, can impact the level of data analysis and comparisons students can explore. Having the data in a digital form can also facilitate its use in additional interdisciplinary study.

◆ Lesson 2: *Essay Submission*

Content area: English, writing

Synopsis: Blogging's nature—including its short, quick, and "easy" content posts—does not lend itself well to the types of organized, planned writing that high school English teachers ask students to develop. Wiki pages are used in this lesson to collect and develop expository essays. Often enough in the classroom, the premium of time restricts students from being able to study one another's writings. With the wiki, students can not only read one another's work, but also analyze the writing of their peers with the intent to discover what makes a better essay. By linking to superlative student work, a teacher can use the open, editable format of wiki pages to organize further classroom discussions and activities.

Standards: NCTE: 4, 8, 12

NETS•S: 1.b, 2.a, b

Age: Grades 5–12. The writing prompts used at upper grade levels might incorporate other subject areas and standards.

Objectives: Students will develop the skills of communicating clearly through the expository essay, ideally enlightening the reader with new information. Students will study other student work to discover writing qualities that both grab and engage the reader's attention. Students will respond to writing prompts and post their writings electronically on a wiki-based server for feedback from the instructor and peers.

Resources: word processor, wiki-based Web server, including a course management system that includes a wiki module (i.e., Moodle), writing prompts, expository lesson ideas (www.Webenglishteacher. com/expwriting.html)

Procedure:

1. The instructor will read an example of a superlative expository essay to students. The instructor then questions the students about what they learned from the essay and what kind of organization was used to present the information.

2. On the wiki, the instructor will use student feedback to develop a resource list, including

hyperlinks for additional writing techniques and mechanics for expository writing. This can include form considerations (sequence, question-answer, comparison, cause-effect, etc.), grammar, vocabulary, and the defined goals of expository writing. This homepage will also link to individual wiki pages for each student's own essay(s), as well as to a page of writing prompts.

3. The writing prompts may include the following:

   a. The best thing you ever ate: What was it? Why was it so good? What other senses contributed to your recollection of this food or meal?

   b. The most difficult sport must be? Support your argument for why your choice of sport is difficult or demanding.

   c. The qualities that make a great piece of music are? What are the elements of a song? Which of these matter to you most? What example songs support the qualities you identify?

   d. We all get help in life. Tell us about a significant event in your life where someone's help made a difference.

   e. Since the dawn of man, technology (in its various forms) has played an important role in the advancement of civilization. What technologies were important to Americans around 1910? Do we think about these technologies now?

   f. Transportation, for work or for recreation, has a high price today. What might be some solutions to the costs of transportation that take place in your lifetime?

4. Students choose a prompt and develop their essay in a word processor. Both drafts and final edits are posted to the wiki.

5. The instructor reviews student essay drafts and appends comments at the bottom of each wiki page.

6. Students read selected student essays from the wiki. Students are asked to annotate the essays with a positive comment about the writing, as well as with a question to the author about his or her writing.

7. Students review their teacher's and peers' comments and revise their essays, if necessary.

8. The instructor leads a class discussion of essay comments, and the students exchange ideas for what made for effective essay writing. These "rules" are then posted on the wiki's front page.

Assessment: Student participation in this lesson will be evaluated with the following rubric:

1. Did the posted, final essay follow the guidelines of an expository essay?

2. Did the essay address the writing prompt and use acceptable grammatical conventions?

3. Did the student provide a question and a positive comment on the assigned readings of other student essays?

4. Did the student participate in classroom discussions?

Notes: This lesson changes the dynamics of writing because students have access to one another's writing. This guaranteed audience motivates students to try their best. This motivating factor can also be used to the instructor's advantage, when directing students to *engage* their audience. This skill can be developed further at higher grade levels.

The technological component here—posting student writing on a Wiki—can be used in a variety of lessons and subject areas. Wiki pages for each student can be used to manage a research project or to post conversations in a foreign language. For some teachers, the most unnerving aspect of a wiki is the fact that *anyone* can make changes to the content of any page. The Instiki wiki engine uses an honor system by asking the author or editor of a page to post their name, but it remains that anyone can still write anything to a wiki.

MediaWiki can be configured to force unique logins for each student, thereby leaving a "trail" of each student's edits and posts. A content management system such as Moodle (which uses a wiki module) can also record each student's changes to the wiki, identified by their login credentials.

Lesson 3: *Developing a Classroom Constitution*

Content area: Social studies

Synopsis: What if the classroom were an Island Country? To understand the history behind the U.S. Constitution and the importance such a document has on our society, students will use a wiki to develop their own constitution for their classroom. Students can cite primary sources for the basis of their new "government." Students within one class can develop their own document, or smaller groups within a class can each be assigned a document.

Standards: NCSS: V, VI, X

NETS•S: 1.a; 2.a, b, d; 3.b, c; 5.d

Age: Grades 7–8

Objectives: Students will develop a classroom "constitution," based on the U.S. Constitution. Through the collaborative development of this document, they will recognize the major components and design of the United States Constitution through emulation. The instructor is encouraged to use this document as part of classroom procedure. Students will be assessed using a rubric that is distributed on the wiki at the start of the project.

Resources: Web-based wiki server, graphic organizer, Inspiration software, rubric

Procedure:

1. The instructor posts to the wiki server the rubric required for ratification of their constitution. The front page points to each "section" as pages on the wiki server: Articles I–VII, amendments, and the preamble. The seventh article of the constitution shall read: "This constitution will be ratified by consensus between your teacher, _____ and principal _____ when the sixth article, covering legal status, is completed by the authors." The sixth amendment contains the rubric for the project.

2. Students receive a graphical organizer for their project. Students draw iconic representations for each block in the organizer (legislative, executive, etc.) or use a graphics program to supply the icons.

3. Students are split into groups to work on the various sections of the class constitution: Article I, Article II,

Article III, Article IV, and Article V. The class begins by collectively drafting a preamble, which will guide each independent group. The preamble should give a title to the country and outline what principles the country (classroom) is guided by. Students refer to the U.S. Constitution and other current and historical documents.

4. The instructor demonstrates the use of the wiki by publishing the preamble.

5. Students work independently on establishing the five articles, comparing the model of the U.S. Constitution. The articles should be written in standard paragraph format. The articles get published onto the wiki by students.

6. Each student group reviews the work of others on the five articles.

7. Students draft proposed amendments as a large group, based on what might have been left out, or what rights students feel they should have in their classroom/country.

8. Students review the document on the wiki. Students consider the sixth article. Have all the requirements been met to make this a legal document (e.g., have they been assessed by the instructor)?

9. The checklist from the sixth article is annotated on the wiki. The principal and teacher approve the constitution in a statement appended to the seventh article.

10. Students practice operating under their new rules in the classroom. Time is appointed for passing laws (rules), following article I, and for settling disputes (article III).

Assessment: The instrument used here to assess student participation in this project measures their fulfillment of the needs required for a classroom constitution. It will be included as Article VI in their wiki.

Article VI: Legal Status

The constitution will only be considered legal and effective if the following criteria are met.

1. The constitution describes how classroom rules are established. (Article I)

2. The constitution describes the officials who make the classroom rules and how these officials are so-named. (Article I)

3. The constitution identifies the executive leader(s) of the classroom, their powers, and their term of office. (Article II)

4. The constitution identifies the relationships among the executive leader(s) and the other two branches of government. (Can the leader[s] influence classroom rules or dispute these rules?) (Article II)

5. The constitution describes judiciary procedure. (How are conflicts resolved?) (Article III)

6. The constitution prepares for contingencies when judiciary procedures are challenged.

(e.g., what happens when a decision requires higher consultation?) (Article III)

7. The constitution describes the procedure for annexing other classrooms into their own, and how that is handled. (Article IV)

8. The constitution describes a procedure for amending the constitution. (Article V)

9. The constitution includes a series of basic rights that students have in the classroom, citing precedents used in U.S. or other world governments.

10. The authors of the constitution work collaboratively together in a speedy and efficient manner.

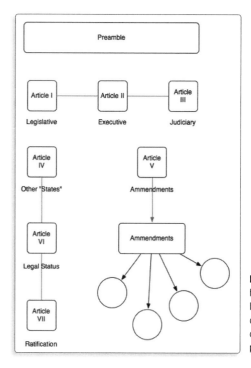

Figure 10.1 This organizer helped me design the lesson, and it can help students grasp the big picture of what they are to accomplish through the wiki.

Notes: This lesson centers around building understanding of the United States Constitution and its basic design. This lesson (adopting a new constitution for an imaginary country) can also be adopted by more advanced social-science courses at the high school level. The wiki enables collaboration between students. It can also enable comparison of the work between different classes.

◈ Lesson 4: *Solving Real-World Math Problems*

Content area: Mathematics, English (language arts)

Synopsis: Word problems and puzzles in math can simulate real-world applications of math. The difficult part for children is translating the "word" problem into the language of mathematics. In this lesson, students consider real-world situations, devise a word problem, and post this problem to a wiki page. They also link the page to another that shows the solution. In the end, they have approached the problem of translating words into math and vice versa.

Standards: NCTM: Measurement, Problem-Solving, Numbers and Operations, Communication.
NETS•S: 1.a, 2.b, 4.b

Age: Grades 4–5

Objectives: Students write a scene between two characters that involves issues of time, money, or size. Within the narrative, they create a problem requiring a computational solution. Students develop an understanding of the relationship between language and mathematics in the creation of their word puzzle.

Resources: wiki server, paper, pencil, resource sheet (resource can be loaded onto the wiki server on its own dedicated page)

Procedure:

1. With guidance from the instructor, students follow a word problem that models what they will create. Through group discussion, students work out the problem, decoding the language and mathematical formulas used.

2. Students are asked to consider a scene between two characters in a story:
   "The characters live in a world where everything is measured and counted exactly: money, time, weight, and the size of objects around them. Create a very-short story that describes an issue with money, time, weight, or the size of objects, and ask the reader to solve a puzzle with these items."

3. Students consult the resource sheet that lists words used in math problems and what the translation means (e.g., increased by = addition; difference between = subtraction; product of = multiplication; out of = division), and they formulate a puzzle following the model used to start the lesson.

4. Students work out the solution to their puzzle.

5. Students post the word problem on their own wiki page.

6. Students link to a new wiki page that shows the solution.

7. Students post the solution to their problem (in numbered steps) on the wiki's answer page.

8. Students practice decoding their word problems by visiting one another's wiki pages.

Assessment: A rubric is used to assess students based on the following criteria:

☐ The word problem is successfully posted on a wiki page.

☐ The solution is successfully posted on a wiki page.

☐ The problem and solution are linked within the wiki.

☐ The problem is presented in the form of a story.

☐ The problem includes specific figures and associated units (e.g., 50 cents, 3/4 of a pound, 1/2 hour, 15 minutes, 50 grams, etc.).

☐ The problem introduces figures that may contribute "noise" (e.g., numbers are introduced that have no bearing on the solution to the problem).

☐ The problem makes correct use of mathematical concepts translated into words (e.g., "less than," "more than," "what percent," etc.).

Notes: Word problems presented in class sometimes include language or details that can confuse decoding the real mathematical problem. Students who prepare word problems for their peers are not likely to use distracting elements in the puzzles. This lesson may be used between different age groups (for example, where older students create word problems for younger students). While this lesson is focused on elementary mathematics, it could also be adapted for more complex problems and puzzles. The real work is coming up with a puzzle and also defining the steps required to solve it.

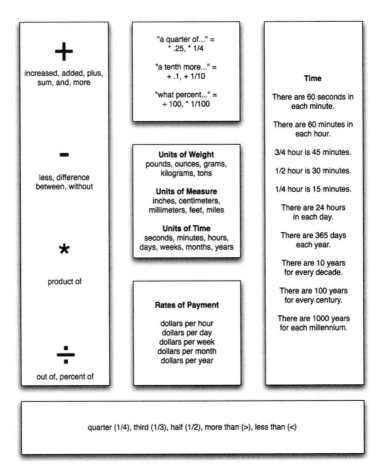

Figure 10.2 This is an example worksheet that can be used to assist students in developing their own word problems.

Lesson 5: *Choices-Based Story*

Content area: English, writing

Synopsis: A popular book series for young readers, *Choose Your Own Adventure,* brings readers into a story and invites them to interact with the story. Depending on choices presented by the author, the reader then turns to different pages within the book, following a unique path that customizes the sequence of events. In this lesson, students construct their own version of a *Choose Your Own Adventure* story, using wiki links that take readers to the next "page" and "challenge" within the story.

Standards: NCTE: 1, 2, 3, 4, 5, 8

NETS•S: 1.a, b, c, d; 2.a, b, d; 5.b; 6.a, b

Age: Grades 10–12

Objectives: Students will use a graphical organizer to organize a story (with multiple courses of action) into small mini-chapters. Students will present the story on a wiki server, linking the various story segments (mini-chapters) together, lending an interactive, first-person role to the reader.

Resources: Inspiration software, wiki server, *Choose Your Own Adventure* titles (Chooseco, www.cyoa.com)

Procedure:

1. The class discusses the styles and techniques used in *Choose Your Own Adventure.* If the class has never encountered this genre of book, classroom time may be spent reading some titles from the series to get a better idea of how they "work."

2. Students pre-write the story by presenting a one- to two-page draft, outlining the environment for the character(s), the perils in this environment, and the types of choices that can be made. With instructor approval, they move on.

3. Students construct a graphical organizer (using paper or Inspiration software) to plan their stories. Students may choose to diagram the sequence of their choices

directly from examples they have read, or they can use a sample graphic organizer.

4. Students write the story segments into the wiki.

5. Students link the story segments in the wiki.

6. Students read other student stories and critique the stories on a Review wiki page (which is linked by the instructor for peer feedback).

Assessment: The stories are assessed in three stages: the pre-writing scenario (30%), the graphic organizer (25%), and the peer review (45%). The peer reviews should address the following questions:

1. Did the story grab my interest? Why or why not?

2. Might the story grab the interest of a younger audience? Why or why not?

3. Did the links work to produce a customized story from beginning to end?

4. Examining the story in detail, did one (or more) segment(s) have more than one input or output path?

5. On a scale of 1–5, how creative were the story and the possible choices?

Notes: In a world of hypertext, this style of story has a lot of possibilities. By enabling students to construct their own organizers, stories of great complexity can be developed. Critical-thinking skills are required to well-organize the story, and students should be encouraged to use cross-branching in their story design (to re-use segments). In the example organizer that follows (Fig. 10.3), cross-branching takes place in several areas. But might some segments cross levels? (e.g., Introduction—Branch 1—Branch 1-A, Branch 2—Branch 2-C, Branch 2-C2, Branch 1-B2, Branch 1-Ending).

This lesson uses the wiki as an assessment instrument, too, by allowing a student's peers to drop comments about the stories in the same online space. The logic required to write these stories is suitable for older students, but you may direct the audience to a younger age group and allow, say, fifth- or sixth-grade students to assess the wiki-hosted stories.

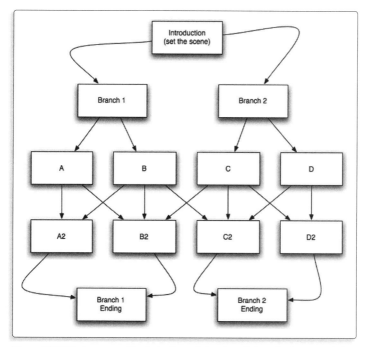

Figure 10.3 This is one possible design for a choices-based story. Students can design their own template or use one based on a book. This template should be used in the assessment of the wiki project, faithfully recording which sections are linked, and how.

CONCLUSION

These lessons were designed to illustrate just a few ways you might employ the use of wiki-based Web sites in your classroom. Wikis are a simple, yet powerful concept that are finding their way into companies as a means for collaboration, documentation, and resource-sharing. In the classroom, wikis take on similar roles. From a knowledge base to a choices-infused story, a wiki allows students to share content one page at a time.

CHAPTER 11

Podcasts in the Classroom

"Podcasting" was declared the 2005 Word of the Year by the editors of the *New Oxford American Dictionary* (2005), which defines the term as "a digital recording of a radio broadcast or similar program, made available on the Internet for downloading to a personal audio player."

One of the most powerful things we can do for students who create original work is to validate their efforts by giving them an audience. One of the great rewards for professional writers and creators is knowing someone is using, reading, or consuming their work. Imagine how this makes the work done by students more exciting, authentic, and real.

Among the easiest ways to publish work is through the Internet. On the Web, everyone who cares to be an author, creator, and publisher can author, create, and publish. It stands to reason that podcasting is an ideal mechanism for students to share their work, and it makes learning more real. We are no longer limited by plain text on the Web. Student publishers can publish a variety of content online, including audio and video podcasts.

"Often, these real-world experiences inspire students to take their assignments more seriously, whether future projects are done for community members or for teachers at school" (Looney, 2005, p. 58).

BEFORE YOU START

1. When publishing anything online, make sure the content you publish is not protected by copyright. If you are publishing content, it ought to be created by you or by colleagues within your organization.

2. Be careful about identifying students when publishing their work. Podcasting school content should not put students at risk or jeopardize their privacy. Ensure that content being published via a podcast is within the bounds of your school's Acceptable Use Policy (AUP).

3. When in doubt, keep your content short and simple—clear and concise. Your stakeholders (students, parents, and colleagues) are already being bombarded with content from every direction. Concise communication of content in manageable "chunks" will likely work best.

4. Do not attempt the impossible overnight. Start slow by gradually adopting these emerging technologies and using them in your day-to-day life. Ongoing practice is required to understand the benefits of some new technologies—including podcasting.

5. Before you become a content publisher, become a content subscriber. To fully understand the RSS technology behind podcasting, subscribe to RSS feeds of interest and podcasts of interest before you try creating your own.

ACCEPTABLE USE POLICIES

Before anyone in your school embarks on a podcasting, blogging, or publishing endeavor, check with school officials about your current computer used policies. With emerging technologies all around us, current policies may not do enough to protect children.

Your Acceptable Use Policy (AUP) should make provisions for what types of content can and cannot be published. This will likely cover content published on school-owned servers, but also content published through school-owned networks. Permission from parents should be requested and granted (some schools also give parents an opt-out option) before publishing student work (including, but not limited to, the student's photos and audio or video recordings of the respective student).

The AUP should state that a) the students' full-names will not be used in any of the Web pages, podcasts, or weblogs; b) student pictures will not be published with personal identifying information such as age or full name; and c) students may not publish any type of text, audio, or video that would put them at risk (including, but not limited to, information on home address, phone number, e-mail address, a place of employment, or any other type of contact information). A statement regarding the quality of work published online should also be included in the AUP, so that work published by administrators, teachers, and students projects a positive, professional image and reflects well on the school(s) or district.

An AUP for technology use in schools should be written considering that in the dharma of publication, authors of content each have their own experiences, beliefs, expertise, naiveté, and agendas. While podcasting and blogging are emerging, exciting, and dynamic technologies for communication, I advise teachers to incorporate these technologies into their instruction under the umbrella of school and/or district support, with policies to handle Web-based and Internet-based communications.

In a recent article by Doug Johnson (n.d.), entitled "Rules for Pod People and a Proposal for Banning Pencils," Johnson postulates that we ought to ban pencils in education for the same reasons that some schools and districts have cited for banning the use of emerging technologies. "A student might write a dirty word or, worse yet, a threatening note to another student, with a pencil," he writes. With tongue-in-cheek wit, Johnson reminds us "each of these technologies has the potential for misuse." The difference with regard to blogging and podcasting is, of course, the inherently wider (potential) audience.

Misuse of these new communications media will undoubtedly take place, either by accident or by intent. I have seen evidence of teachers who posted content before thinking through all the consequences of their blogs; principals who have sent out terse e-mails before they understood the big picture; and students who have tested the boundaries of acceptable content. Having a clear AUP in place helps everyone understand why the technology is being provided and what policies govern its use. When such an AUP exists and is enforced, technology can be used just as safely and securely as a pencil.

STUDENT PODCASTING

In chapter 3 we examined some guidelines for creating podcasts. We will reiterate those guidelines in the following examples. I have separated these two sections on podcasting because the outcome of podcasting in the classroom with students differs from that done by teachers and administrators. Podcasting teachers and administrators are primarily concerned with increasing communication into the homes of students and the community. This is a noble endeavor, and educator-podcasters are better prepared to approach classroom pod-casting with students when they have already had the experience with technical issues and feedback that comes from self-publishing.

Podcasting for students in the classroom is a worthwhile project for two principal reasons. One, the thrill of having their original content available to netizens both familiar and unfamiliar to the students is an exciting, motivating prospect. This is especially so when coupled with other students' collaborative exercises (in a different setting, location, or age group). Knowing you have an audience of peers that will proffer feedback helps students focus on the final product. "When you're writing an essay, you don't try your hardest because after you're done, you throw it away or put it in a box...now we try a lot harder [with podcast writing], because we want other people to know that we [can] do more. We want people to hear us." (Borja, 2005)

The second reason podcasting offers students a valuable learning experience is because of the requisite planning, writing, and organization that podcasts demand. Students who podcast are writing, considering, and manipulating content within formal structures. They are collaborating with adults and classmates alike, planning and practicing. When classroom podcasting activities are focused on content standards, students also have the opportunity to learn concepts through research and production—often evaluating, synthesizing, and analyzing the content of their (and others') podcast episodes. Student podcasters are also using modern authoring techniques that catapult them into a society embracing new economic frontiers brought about by globalization and collaborative benefits.

PODCASTING IN THE CLASSROOM

◆ **Lesson 1:** *School News*

Content area: English, technology

Synopsis: Students will act as reporters to collect information important to teachers and fellow students, and act as broadcasters to publish this information as a podcast for the school. Some schools may elect to do this on a daily basis; others, on a weekly basis.

Standards: NCTE: 4, 7, 8, 12
NETS•S: 1.b; 2.a, d; 3.a; 4.c; 5.a; 6.a
NETS•T: I.A, V.D

Age: Grades 5–12

Objectives: Students will research identified information of interest to students and teachers from a variety of sources and produce a short, regular podcast show after completing a script worksheet. Students will write a script for the podcast and record the script using a computer. With the assistance of an educator, they will publish the file onto a server.

Resources: multimedia computer, microphone, audio editing software, Web server, script worksheet

Students can be assisted in this exercise (dependent, in part, on their age) with scaffolding provided by the instructor—in the form of a sample, completed project or via a planning worksheet.

There are several phases to this project. The first, collection, is where students find and collect the news to be reported. At the elementary level, this might include announcements from the school office, a weather report, or a quote from a notable personality within the community or school. Many online subscription services (such as online encyclopedias and streaming video services) provide content (e.g., interesting facts and trivia) that can be tied to topics being covered in classes. Students at the elementary level can also, for example, report on the progress of classroom science experiments, discuss performances in the arts at the school, or profile a teacher.

At the secondary level, students can expand the collection of information by becoming more involved. They may conduct interviews with persons of interest or compose news reports over the span of days or weeks. Secondary students can also cover social studies standards by reporting on real-world news events.

Procedure:

1. Two days prior to recording the podcast, students work in small groups (1–4 students) to complete the worksheet that will form the basis for their script. In the example worksheet used here, students are asked to research a) something of interest today; b) something new (e.g., school events or subject-matter-based content); and c) the lunch menu. For the first two sections, students are asked to list their sources of information.

2. One day prior to the podcast, students are asked to write their script, detailing who says what and every word spoken. The introduction and end of the podcast are already included on the worksheet. Students will be putting their researched information into a written format, as seen in this example:

Julie: Good morning! This is Julie and Tong with the Bull-frog News! Tong, what day is today?

Tong: Julie, today is Monday, March 20. Last week, many people were wearing green. Did you celebrate St. Patrick's Day?

Julie: My mom made green cupcakes, but that's about it. Can you guess what the next holiday is on our calendar?

Tong: Would that be April Fool's Day?

Julie: That's right! Be sure to mark your classroom calendars and be prepared if someone plans to play a trick on you.

Tong: Today we have a report from our interview with Mrs. Roberts, who drives bus number five.

Julie: Tong, do you ride the bus to school?

Tong: Julie, I do. I had the opportunity to send a few questions to Mrs. Roberts, who sent us a reply. I learned a lot about her. Who knew bus drivers could be so interesting?

Julie: What did you find out?

Tong: Mrs. Roberts was born in 1967. She has been a bus driver since 1996. She says it takes a lot of skill to drive a bus. She finds it interesting that she's a bus driver, because she never rode the bus when she went to school.

Julie: She didn't? Where did she go to school?

Tong: Mrs. Roberts went to school in South Africa. Can you believe that? She lived next to the school, so she did not need a ride to school. She came to the United States in 1983. She told us that if we ever have the opportunity to go to South Africa, we should. The beaches there are beautiful.

Julie: We'll have to check it out. According to the CIA World Fact Book, South Africa has almost 3,000 kilometers of coastline. That means a lot of beaches. And the British came to South Africa after the Dutch explorers. I guess that is why Mrs. Roberts' accent is so interesting!

Tong: That's right, Julie. I guess now we know: Mrs. Roberts is not from Ireland or Australia. Next time you see her, let her know you learned more about her through our podcast!

Julie: Okay, Tong, I will. And now, today's lunch menu is chicken patties with green beans and carrots. Salads will also be available today.

Tong: Okay, Julie, we hope everyone enjoys lunch and has a great day.

3. Students record the teacher-approved script using a computer and audio-editing software. As students become more proficient at editing digital audio, they may choose to include interstitials (bumpers, sound effects) into the podcast to divide up changes in the format. For instance, before each announcement of the school lunch, a dinner bell sound effect might be inserted into the podcast.

4. Once the podcast is recorded, students will export the audio file into an MP3 format and (with the instructor's assistance) upload the file to a server where it can be accessed by other students or made available on the Web.

Assessment:

1. Was an efficient use of time used to collect information for the podcast?

2. Was the worksheet completed accurately?

3. Were the information sources recorded on the worksheet?

4. Did the written script include good use of grammar, punctuation, and spelling?

5. Was the "talk time" of each participant equal?

6. Was the recorded audio edited to exclude background noise, mistakes, and blank air time?

7. Was the recorded audio exported in a compressed format and labeled appropriately for upload to the server?

Podcast Worksheet

Name(s) of Podcasters: _____ Date: _____

Introduction: Introduce yourself to listeners.

Hello! Today is _____ and this your host _____ with _____. Welcome to our podcast, _____ .

What Happened Yesterday? (What made yesterday unique?)

Sources:

Let's Learn Something New

Sources:

What's For Lunch?

	Special Items:

Closing: Choose a Closing

Have a great day!	The early bird gets the worm!	Remember! Go for the gold in everything you do!
Remember: make a difference today.	Have a good day, and remember thinking is good for you.	Have a good one, and make a friend today.

Figure 11.1 A sample worksheet for this project. Portions of the worksheet provide scaffolding, while others allow placement of completely new content by students. Younger students would likely need to write the content for the middle sections (using complete sentences) before recording the podcast.

Notes: Many variations can take place in this lesson, maintaining the basic idea of information collecting, organization, writing, and recording. The focus of the podcast can change to social studies, for instance, in a school where a focus on improving achievement in social studies is warranted. Collaboration for the podcast can be further explored when different teams are assigned to collect, write, and record the sessions. This lesson was planned to be an ongoing project for a classroom, where the roles of reporter, announcer, and writer can be rotated throughout the school year.

Lesson 2: *Book Review*

Content area: English, reading

Synopsis: Students will create a podcast that takes the book review into the 21st century. Students can be asked to make an enhanced podcast by producing graphics that can be used to depict scenes in the book. The feedback students receive from a potential audience of parents, peers, and teachers elevate this brand of book report. Teachers must demand a student's best work before the podcast is published online. This lesson is enriched when students must work in small groups, to collaborate the planning, writing, artwork production, recording, and editing of the podcast.

Standards: NCTE: 1, 3, 4, 6, 8, 11, 12
Visual Arts (Grades 5–8): 3, 6
NETS•S: 1.a, b; 2.b; 3.a; 4.b

Age: Grades 4–8

Objectives: Students will effectively communicate the characters, plot, and favorite parts of a book they have read. Working toward the production of an enhanced podcast, they will communicate through writing, speech, and creating visual elements such as drawings and photographs.

Resources: multimedia computer with microphone, audio editing software, Inspiration software with template, word processor, scanner or digital camera, Web server for publishing podcast

Reading comprehension has been approached in a variety of ways over the years, and the book report is but one option for teachers. In this lesson, we modernize the standard book report by creating a podcast. I have seen this lesson done with students of all ages, using both audio and video. In this example, we integrate the visual arts standards by producing an enhanced podcast. GarageBand on the Macintosh is the ideal tool for creating enhanced podcasts. Microsoft Photo Story (for Windows) can be used to create a similar product as a video podcast.

If the podcast is published through a weblog that supports comments, other student interpretations and reactions to the book (e.g., favorite parts) can add to the value of the review. Student comments can also be used as part of the assessment of the enhanced podcast review.

Procedure:

1. Students will select a book to read and review this lesson's final assessment rubric.

2. Students will receive a copy of a podcast template for use with Inspiration (software application).

   The graphical template might include the following questions:

   ☐ What is the book's title?

   ☐ Who wrote it?

   ☐ What is one interesting fact about the author?

   ☐ What did you learn by reading this book?

☐ What was the plot of the story?

☐ Where is the book set?

☐ What did you like about this book?

☐ What did you not like about this book?

☐ How would you change what you didn't like (if you could) to improve the book?

☐ Would you recommend this book to others?

3. Students will read the book in a time frame deemed appropriate by the instructor.

4. Students will complete the graphic organizer template using Inspiration.

5. Students will generate a series of images to be used in the podcast. (These could reproduce scenes from the book or depict the story's setting.)

6. Students will digitize the artwork (produced for the review) by using a flatbed scanner or a digital camera.

7. Using a word processor and their graphic organizer, students will write a script for their book review podcast. The format must include all the elements noted in the objective, and creativity is encouraged. Students may, for instance, include quotes from characters in the book using voice characterizations or inflections that match what they might imagine the characters to sound like.

8. Students record their written review using editing software. The scanned/photographed artwork is added to create an enhanced podcast.

9. Students export the podcasts in a compressed format for publication.

10. Teachers publish approved podcasts to a blog.

11. Other students are invited to comment on the podcasts of their peers, adding their own comments about, say, their own interpretation of the books.

Assessment: The included rubric is used to assess the final product. Instructors may assess the project in stages (planning in Inspiration, written script, artwork, audio podcast), and include the comments of peers in evaluating the project.

Notes: This lesson can be done with or without the added artwork piece. The complexity of the lesson obviously needs to adapt to the students' grade level. Students in the area targeted (Grades 4–8) can edit an enhanced podcast. The focus of the podcast, along with the rubric, can be tailored to a specific class group. This lesson can be used with high school students as well, and the complexity of the project can be increased accordingly. I envision high school students doing a project like this with video and adding theatrical elements and dramatizations.

The benefits of publishing online (where others can see the students' work) cannot be undervalued. A colleague of mine (teaching ninth-grade social studies) each year asks his honors students to read several books throughout the year. They published written reviews of their books on Amazon.com. While far simpler than producing an enhanced podcast, the simple act of adding one's input to a collective body of reviews was a rewarding experience for the students.

Rubric : Book Report Podcast

Student Name: _____

CATEGORY	4	3	2	1
Presentation	Well-rehearsed with smooth delivery that holds audience attention.	Rehearsed with fairly smooth delivery that holds audience attention most of the time.	Delivery not smooth, but able to maintain interest of the audience most of the time.	Delivery not smooth and audience attention often lost.
Audio Quality	Music, effects, and voices are clear and well-understood by the listener.	Relatively well-understood by the listener, minor defects in editing.	Delivery not smooth, and portions of the podcast are difficult to understand or hear.	Delivery not smooth a major portion of the podcast is misunderstood, isn't listener-friendly, or lacks content related to the report.
Content - Facts	Covers book facts in-depth including book title, author, author fact, book setting, and story plot. Subject knowledge is excellent.	Includes essential knowledge about the book and author. Subject knowledge appears to be good.	Includes essential information about the book and author but there are 1-2 factual errors, or information is missing.	Content is minimal OR there are several factual errors.
Book Opinions	Opinions about the book, including likes and dislikes, are communicated well.	Opinions about the book are communicated within the podcast.	Opinions are not completely stated, or are confusing to understand.	One or fewer opinions are shared about the book.
Recommendation	The podcaster(s) chooses to recommend or not recommend this book to others based on a number of clearly stated reasons.	The podcaster(s) chooses to recommend or not recommend the book to others, but the reasons behind the opinion were not clearly stated.	The podcaster(s) gives an opinion about their preference for the book but does not provide reasons.	The recommendation is never included in the podcast.
Mechanics	No grammatical errors is misspoken English.	Three mechanical/speech errors.	Four mechanical/grammatical/speech errors.	More than 4 errors.
What did you learn?	The podcaster(s) clearly shares something they learned from the content/reading of this book.	The podcaster(s) shares something they learned through reading this book.	Something learned is shared, but is confusing or misunderstood.	The podcaster(s) does not include what they learned from reading the book.
Group Work	Each member of the group contributed something significant to the final product.	The majority of members within the group contributed to the quality of the final product.	Half of the group contributed to the final product.	Only one person made a significant contribution towards the final product.

Figure 11.2: A rubric is a wise option for assessing multimedia projects. Students can also be asked to rate themselves and others with the same instrument.

While I recommend using a graphical-style organizer for students to dump information and their opinions about the book, one isn't required. It can be used, however, as part of the enhanced podcast in the sections where students are not displaying artwork. Inspiration software easily lets students export their document into a graphic file that can be included alongside the scanned or photographed scenes from the book.

◆ Lesson 3: *Unit Summary Podcast*

Content area: Science (This lesson example can be adapted to any content area and just about any content standard.)

Synopsis: A select group of students transforms a unit of study into a podcast. Throughout the year, each student in a classroom will participate in at least one of these productions. The finished podcast becomes a review instrument for other students and classes in the school or district.

Standards: NSES: Physical Science (K–4)
NETS•S: 1.a, d; 2.a, b, d; 3.b, 5.b, d; 6.b

Age: Grades 4–6

Objectives: Students will create an audio podcast organized in five major sections that covers the principles behind electricity, as defined by the school's science curriculum. Using an organizational framework supplied by the instructor, topics will include characteristics of conductors and insulators, basic circuits, static electricity, and the ability of electrical energy to be transformed into heat, light, and mechanical energy. Also included are the principles of simple electromagnets and the historical contributions made toward understanding electricity.

Students will be evaluated on their ability to grasp the major points of study in the unit (summarization), and on their ability to clearly communicate these concepts through the podcast medium.

Resources: science textbook, multimedia computer with microphone, podcast planning packet, unit worksheets, media resources.

Procedure:

1. Introduce the project to the podcasting group of students. Before they begin, they need to understand the five major sections of the podcast. These are: Introduction, Teaser, Did You Know?, Web Watch, and Creative Corner. The instructor divides the group and assigns responsibilities for each of the podcast's five sections.

2. Students work with their classroom resources to complete the podcast planning packet with content from the unit on electricity. Students maintain a checklist of the major components of the standards-content to ensure each item on the checklist is included in the podcast planning.

3. Students rehearse the content they create using the packet.

4. The instructor reviews and approves the content for the podcast. If needed, students make necessary revisions to the script.

5. Students record and edit the podcast, using the packet as a guide.

6. The instructor assesses the podcast and uploads a compressed version of the recording to a server for others to listen.

This five-sectioned podcast works well with a group of four students. In this scenario, each student is assigned one of the podcast's five sections and is responsible for supplying the material required to complete the worksheet in the podcast planning packet. The host's role is to introduce the podcast at the beginning, thank listeners at the end, and write the teaser. The host may also participate in a dialogue with other students in other sections/segments of the recording.

Interstitials (a "bumper" or audio cue between two sections of a podcast) are a fun additional element that students can insert between the podcast's five sections. You may instruct students to use the

Unit Study Planning Packet

Unit Title: _____

This packet includes worksheets for five sections of the podcast:

Section	Student
Introduction	
Teaser	
Did You Know?	
Web Watch	
Creative Corner	

Rubric

	Well Done (5)	Mostly (3)	Lacking (1)
Does the podcast follow the script outlined in this packet?			
Did you complete your packet worksheet in a timely manner?			
Did you accurately summarize the concepts?			
Is the audio in the podcast clear and easy to hear?			
Did you cover conductors and insulators?			
Basic circuits?			
Static electricity?			
Transformation of electric energy into heat?			
Electromagnets?			
Historical milestones in electricity?			

Figure 11.3 The worksheets in this packet can be used to facilitate the creation of a podcast about a particular unit of study.

same sound effects (called "stingers") in each podcast to identify the major sections.

Assessment: Because the product of this lesson is a podcast, we will again use a rubric to evaluate the product.

Group Concerns:

- ☐ Was the audio clear and were words easy to hear?

- ☐ Did the podcast follow the script provided in the planning packet?

- ☐ Did students address the major concepts dealing with electricity, including characteristics of conductors and insulators, basic circuits, static electricity; ability of electrical energy to be transformed into heat, light, and mechanical energy; simple electromagnets; historical contributions?

Individual Concerns:

- ☐ Did you complete your section in the allotted time?

- ☐ Did you accurately summarize the concepts covered in this unit of study?

Notes: This lesson essentially guided us through producing a podcast centered on a large unit of study. This unit can include an almost infinite number of variations. It can be used beyond the grade levels identified here and for any content area. Marzano's strategies of note-taking and frequent summarization in the classroom (Marzano, Pickering, & Pollock, 2004) can help students with identifying key concepts of study for inclusion in their podcast.

This lesson was inspired by the group podcasts produced at Willowdale Elementary School in Omaha, Nebraska (available online at www.mpsomaha.org/willow/radio/listen.html).

Learning in Hand offers PDF templates used to produce the *Radio WillowWeb* podcasts (www.learninginhand.com/podcasting/ RadioWillowWeb.pdf).

Lesson 4: *Career Interview Podcasts*

Content area: Guidance, career preparation, business education

Synopsis: Too many students today are unaware of all the career opportunities available to them upon leaving high school and college. Guidance counselors may take interest in this lesson, which challenges students to explore future careers by interviewing a number of professionals in the workplace.

Standards: NBEA Career Development: II, V, VI
NETS•S: 1.b, c; 2.a, b; 3.a; 4.a, c; 5.a, d

Age: Grades 8–10

Objectives: Using investigative reporting techniques, students will interview members of the professional community, using voice recorders (or MP3 players coupled with microphones), to discover details about different jobs and career paths. Students will publish these interviews as audio podcasts to form a body of information accessible online by other students considering a variety of careers.

Resources: digital voice recorder, multimedia computer, audio editing software, pool of professional interviewees

In this lesson, less emphasis is on formal interviewing technique, and more emphasis is on collecting authentic information students might use in considering various careers. The instructor for this lesson will need to facilitate the scheduling of working professionals willing to participate. In some schools, this can be scheduled around a career or job fair. In arranging interviews, instructors should develop an informative release form that gives each person interviewed an idea of what they are contributing to, what time commitment is expected, and notification that the interview will be placed online. The instructor should arrange for the interviews to be done on school grounds under the supervision of the instructor or school staff.

Alternatively, students may desire to interview their parents and family members at home, using the school's voice recorder.

Procedure:

1. As a class group, students will develop a pool of interview questions that can be used with a wide variety of interviewees. These may include questions about:

   ☐ the education required to do the job,

   ☐ the number of years' experience required for the job,

   ☐ the number of hours worked each day/week,

   ☐ what is liked best about the job,

   ☐ what is liked least about the job,

   ☐ where this profession is headed in the future,

   ☐ what subjects in high school helped best prepare the interviewee for their current position.

2. Students will interview professionals in the community about their career. Each interview should

identify the student conducting the interview, as well as the name of the professional being interviewed. Students may add specific questions to the interview. Students will record the interview with a digital voice recorder.

3. If editing is required, students will edit the interviews on the computer using sound-editing software.

4. Compressed versions (MP3, AAC) of the interviews will be passed to the instructor for assessment, and then published as an ongoing podcast project on the Web.

5. Once interviews are complete and published, students are asked to write a one-page reflection on what they learned from listening to their class-created podcasts. They can address what careers are of interest to them, and which careers they might be considering before and after the project.

Assessment: There are two parts to this lesson. The interview podcast, and the post-interview reflection. I recommend assessing these components separately.

Rubrics can be used to assess both sections. The first instrument should consider:

☐ Were all the questions developed by the class asked of the interviewee?

☐ Did the student contribute any of his/her own questions to add value to the interview?

☐ Was the interview easy to follow and understand?

☐ At the start of the recording, did the student properly introduce him- or herself, as well as the person being interviewed?

The second rubric should consider:

☐ Does the reflection meet the length requirement?

☐ Does the reflection clearly state what the student learned by listening to the collection of career interviews?

☐ Does the reflection highlight the experience with the professional interviewee?

☐ Does the student reveal what career interests he/she had before and after the project's completion?

Notes: This project can also be done with video cameras to produce video podcasts. Using video will increase the time required for the project. Video can be used, however, to better showcase the working environment of the interviewee.

Blogs can also be used by students to author their reflections on careers. I recommend using a single blog set up for the project, in which each student can contribute. These are called "group" or "community" blogs. The blog can also be used as the publishing medium for the audio podcasts of the interviews.

Using podcasting as an interview medium can be adapted to collect other types of information from individuals (e.g., stronger opinions, personal histories, and personal reactions to historical events, tragedies, and national or international disasters).

◆ Lesson 5: *World Language Conversations*

Content area: World languages

Synopsis: In this lesson, students use the podcast medium and a social photography Web site to develop a conversation between two or more people, conducted in a foreign language. To create an enhanced podcast, students may elect to use the photographs chosen as the basis for the conversation in the podcast.

The Web is already a rich resource for finding content about cultures different than our own. The iTunes podcast directory, alone, is full of language-learning podcasts in audio and video format. This lesson places emphasis on the creation of an original conversation. Students frame the conversation in a foreign language with a native-language description at the podcast's start, and with questions for listeners to answer at the podcast's end.

Standards: ACTFL: 1.1, 1.3, 5.1
NETS•S: 1.a, b; 2.a, b, c; 3.a; 5.a

Age: Grades 7–12

Objectives: Students will analyze a series of photographs depicting action between one or more persons. In small groups, students will develop a plausible conversation in the foreign language that is supported by the photographs. Students will record the conversation as an audio podcast.

Resources: access to a digital photo collection, or to Creative Commons-licensed digital photos (such as Flickr, www.flickr.com), multimedia computer with microphone, audio recording/editing software, software for creating an enhanced podcast

Procedure:

1. With the instructor's assistance, students will select 1–5 digital photos using the Creative Commons search function at flickr.com. Using photos from the "attribution-only" license will enable the photos to be used within the enhanced podcast, and then redistributed on the Web (as long as students cite the photo's attribution).

2. The photos will be studied in small groups of 2 to 3 students. Students will develop a 3- to 4-minute conversation between characters identified in- and outside of the photographs. Students will write or type the conversation for approval.

3. Following the instructor's approval, students will practice the conversation in the foreign language.

4. To guide the listener, students will write an introduction and then develop and write five questions in their native language. A restaurant scene, for example, may start out: "On a hot summer afternoon after work, Marta and Luis meet in a café for a soft drink and a conversation. See if you can figure out what Marta's secret is—what she reveals to Luis." One of the questions following the conversation might include something like: "Luis mentions he has been working for a long time. How many months did he say he worked for Allen Equipment?"

5. Students record the three-part podcast using audio recording software on the computer. Students edit the recording to remove mistakes, empty space, and long pauses.

6. If available, students augment the conversation with the photos used to frame the conversation, including them in the project as an enhanced or video podcast.

7. Students upload the recordings in a compressed format (MP3, AAC) to a Web server. If Creative Commons-licensed photography is used, students note the photo sources in the podcast description, as part of the RSS feed.

8. Students in the class listen to the podcasts, and they answer the questions in a group format.

Assessment: The instructor may require students to use a list of vocabulary words as part of their conversation. If so:

☐ Does the conversation include the vocabulary in the correct context?

☐ Is pronunciation accurate?

☐ Does the conversation follow the photographs well?

☐ Is the podcast easy to follow and understand?

☐ Is the podcast framed with a short description and discussion questions?

☐ Do the photographs used include attribution as part of the podcast file's description?

Notes: Instructors may elect to use photographs taken by themselves or by their students (in place of publicly available photos on Flickr). In lieu of discussing the student-created questions about their dialogues, the instructor may elect to post the podcasts online through a blog, and then invite students to answer the questions in their own blogs (using trackback links to the original podcast/blog post). The answers to the questions delivered in the native language may also be answered in the foreign language, especially with more advanced learners.

CHAPTER 12

Newsfeeds in the Classroom

We finish exploring classroom examples with a return to a focus on RSS. RSS is popping up in a number of useful Web sites that extend beyond blogs, wikis, and podcasts. As technology—and especially Web technology—advances, information literacy changes. One concern for the future of information literacy is to avoid information overload—too much content with too little focus. For all the shuffling, sifting through, evaluating, and distilling of the information that comes to us, our first focus ought to be on information management.

In the classroom examples that follow, we will explore using Web sites for managing photos, news sources, specialized blogs, and even word processors, which are all involved in RSS. RSS organizes the influx of information we subscribe to. We have already seen how this technology can help us manage student and teacher bloggers. It is now time to explore how RSS can be used with content produced by a world of other content creators and prosumers.

RSS will likely be a technology that students will later use for both work and pleasure. "Students who can use technology to improve communication and enhance their learning will have an advantage over students lacking those skills…Approaches to teaching must address the reality that we live in a world filled with rich visuals and audio, communicated over many digital devices…" (Looney, 2005, p.58).

◆ Lesson 1: *Plugin to the News*

Content area: Social studies, current events

Synopsis: Using a newsreader/aggregator and the online service *news.yahoo.com*, students will construct a timeline, documenting key events in an emerging news story of local, national, or international interest.

Standards: NCSS: II, III

            NETS•S: 3.b, c; 4.c; 5.c; 6.a, b

Age: Grade 6–12 (Secondary)

Objectives: Students will use technology to facilitate the construction of a summary of an online, emerging story in the news. Students will use critical evaluation skills to construct the summary as the story accumulates from different sources and over time. Students will be assessed by the quality of their summary presentation and their ability to combine disparate perspectives from various news sources.

Resources: Students will use a desktop-based news aggregator, such as RSS Reader (Windows) or NetNewsWire Lite (Macintosh), in addition to a Web browser and a word processor. Additional Web sites (such as www.teach-nology.com/web_tools/materials/timelines/) and software (such as Tom Snyder Productions' TimeLiner, Microsoft PowerPoint, Inspiration or the online tool Gliffy [www.gliffy.com]) may be used to construct their summary.

Procedure:

1. In a group environment, students will use Google News (http://news.yahoo.com) with an instructor to survey current news stories.

2. Students will distill current stories into more generalized topics. For example, if various news stories

report record-high temperatures, the generalized topic might be called "Warming Trend." Or, if various stories report on a debate between the president and congress, the generalized topic might become "Presidential and Congressional Relations." If a story is about a world-record holder, to use yet another example, the topic might become "World Record Achieved." Finally, if a story is about a favorite company or personality, the topic would center on that organization or individual. Classroom time can be used to practice distilling specific stories to more generalized topics.

3. Students will establish a topic for the project. It is likely to fall under the heading of current events.

4. Next, students will conduct a search on their topic at Google News.

5. Students will use the RSS newsfeed link on their search-results page to copy the RSS link, and then paste the link as a subscription in their news aggregator.

6. Students next begin tracking the news by journaling aspects of the emerging news stories on a weekly basis. They make a note of significant dates using the news aggregator and of the topic-related writing using a word processor or text editor.

7. Once the period of investigation has concluded, as established by the instructor (two months or more is recommended), students begin to analyze their journal of stories: What are the major events? When did they take place? How might a description of what happened over the entire period differ from what took

place in one news story? Were there details in different news stories that contradicted one another? What surprised students about their news topic? What did they learn from following this topic over a period of time? What might happen next?

8. After students have analyzed their topic—seen through the lens of their collected news stories—they will construct a timeline of important milestones in the topic's history. Students can use software to facilitate the construction of their timeline.

9. Next, students will present the findings of their research by answering the following questions in a format deemed acceptable by the instructor (PowerPoint, photo slide show, digital movie, TimeLiner presentation, etc.): What topic did I cover? What news stories did I initially find that helped me decide on this topic? What happened over time as I kept watch on this topic? Who are the individuals responsible for how the story has evolved? What stayed the same as this story unfolded? What impact does this topic/story have for other people?

10. Participating students hearing presentations should prepare one question that the presenter ought to be able to answer based on their research into their topic.

Assessment: Students will be evaluated on:

1. Did you consistently use time on task to evaluate the latest news reports using a news aggregator during allotted class time?

2. Did you address the major questions (Procedure 9) in your presentation?

3. Did your timeline accurately portray major events in the topic you followed?

4. Did your investigation reveal various points of view by reporters or individuals in the news reports? If so, did you share these with your audience?

Notes: This lesson can also be administered using Google News (http://news.google.com). Many online sources, such as the *New York Times* (www.nytimes.com/services/xml/rss/) offer RSS feeds for pre-determined categories of news (technology, business, world events, etc.).

Lesson 2: *Popularity of Extreme Sports*

Content area: Physical education, technology, journalism

Synopsis: Using a news aggregator, students will track what's popular and notable about extreme sports through the Digg Web site (http://dig.com). Students will choose one or more stories of interest to teach others about a particular extreme sport, backed with critical Web research using a general search engine.

Standards: NASPE (Physical Education): 2, 6
NCTE (English): 8, 12
NETS•S: 1.a, d; 2.b; 3.b; 5.a

Age: Grades 9–12 (Some stories that appear on Digg may not be suitable for all ages. Instructors may wish to preview the newsfeed before students begin the project.)

Objectives: Students will use Web resources to explore an extreme sport, learning all about how a particular sport (or game) is performed (or played). Students will apply critical research skills to determine if sites similar to Digg are reliable sources of information. Students will be assessed by the successful completion of a Web site evaluation form and their ability to successfully communicate why the story (and sport) found through Digg was/is popular. Students will also be assessed on the details they provide about the extreme sport, including what the game is about, what the rules are, whether there are professional players, what specialized equipment are required, and where spectators have the opportunity to watch the sport (or game).

Resources: Web browser for accessing a generalized search engine such as Yahoo!, Google, or Ask.com; news aggregator for following recently popularized stories on the Web from Digg (http://digg.com/rss/indexextreme_sports.xml); and a Web site evaluation form. If your school does not use a standardized form for evaluating Web sites, Joe Barker from the University of California at Berkeley maintains an excellent resource (www.lib.berkeley.edu/TeachingLib/Guides/Internet/Evaluate.html), and Kathy Schrock offers a free checklist (http://school.discovery.com/schrockguide/evalhigh.html).

Procedure:

1. Discuss with students what Web sites like Digg do: They allow online users to vote for online content that is of special interest to them. By voting for a story, Web page, or blog post, Digg users promote that content as worthy of notice by others. A popular story may not be accurate or tell the whole story, but typically includes something of sensational interest.

2. Students subscribe to the newsfeed using a news aggregator: http://digg.com/rss/indexextreme_sports.xml.

3. Students will consider one or two topics of interest from the newsfeed.

4. Students will summarize what comment posters on Digg have to say about the "dugg" story. Comment

posters may include links to other content online. These links should support their position.

5. Students will conduct research (using a search engine) regarding the extreme sport of interest, as explored through the Digg newsfeed. Their resources should help them answer these questions: What is the game/sport called? What is it about? What are the rules for the game/sport? Are there professional players in this game/sport? Who are some of the well-known athletes? What specialized equipment is required to play the game/sport? Where do spectators have the opportunity to watch the game/sport?

6. For each Web site used to answer questions, students will complete a Web site evaluation form. If a Web site fails the test of reliability, then another site should be considered to corroborate the desired content being searched.

7. Students may present their research in a number of ways, including authoring a blog, creating a multimedia presentation, writing a paper, completing a worksheet prepared by the instructor, or writing a story for the school newspaper.

Assessment: Students will be evaluated on the following points (65 point scale):

1. Was the story or stories found via Digg appropriate for school use? (5 points)

2. Did you effectively communicate details regarding the extreme sport described in the Digg story? (30 points)

3. Did the Web sites used for research about the extreme sport evaluate well for reliability? (10 points)

4. Did you effectively communicate what was special about the story or stories on Digg that made it/them popular? (5 points)

5. Were the cited facts regarding the extreme sport you researched supported with Web page URLs, and were the Web site evaluation forms for each of these sources filled-out completely and accurately? (15 points)

Notes: To integrate critical research skills, this lesson can be adopted for a variety of journalism topics in newspapers, electronic journals, and blogs. All Digg RSS feeds can be found at: http://digg.com/about-rss.

Lesson 3: *Getting Social with Independent Study*

Social computing is likely something we will hear a lot about soon. *Social* simply implies there is collaboration going on between individuals—sharing a service, content, or both. *Social software* would include things such as discussion boards, video chat, or instant messaging. But this term also includes new breeds of software, such as SubEthaEdit (www.codingmonkeys.de), which lets users on Macintosh network collaborate on a document in real time. Google Docs (http://docs.google.com) also allows for collaborative services on word processing documents. Flickr.com, the site for uploading and sharing photos, is also an example of social software, which enables users to comment on and communicate about shared photographs. The key to understanding social software is in the simple word *share.* Software becomes social when it permits content exchange.

This lesson will integrate the use of a popular Web site with helping track a student's progress in researching a topic for an extended, independent study. It can likewise be used by educators to build shared collections of links for student use.

Netscape calls them "bookmarks," and Internet Explorer calls them "favorites." However, you label the Web sites you set aside, and there is a Read/Write way to keep track of them. del.icio.us (http://del.icio.us/) lets us bookmark favorite Web sites. Instead of a bookmark list living on one computer (as most bookmarks do), your bookmarks are stored on the del.icio.us servers. There is one primary advantage to storing your bookmarks online: they can follow you wherever you go. A second advantage (and sometimes a disadvantage) is that the sharing of Web resources is public: by default, your bookmarks are shared with everyone else online. This means your bookmarks on del.icio.us (by default) are not private. This also means that letting students loose into del.icio.us may turn up links to sites we ought not be visiting while at school.

del.icio.us nevertheless has played an important role in the way we deal with valuable Web content in our school district. For example, the social aspect of my own del.icio.us database means I have a mechanism for sharing bookmarks with other teachers in our district. But we took things one step further. We asked: What if—instead of placing the burden on one person to find Web content of value—we shared the responsibility? So we set up a school-based account, and I shared the username and password with our media specialists and computer lab managers. They regularly identified valuable Web content, and each of them could add content independently of one another in our bookmarks list. And we did not stop there.

Each bookmark in del.icio.us can be tagged. Tags are like keywords: they are an easy-to-use mechanism for identifying a bookmark with one or more labels. To enable a usable system, I established an "approved" keyword list that everyone used: education, elementary, middle, high, math, science, English, social studies, art, music, health, reading, technology, games, WebQuests, research, movies, sounds. You can use any words you like, but we decided on these.

del.icio.us, of course, allows us to search by keyword. By collectively adding bookmarks to del.icio.us, we created a database of best-quality

Web sites that could be searched by a number of keywords. Every teacher in our district could do a search for the keyword, or a combination of keywords, that matched their search needs.

Anyone can browse the del.icio.us bookmarks. To tag and create your own bookmark list, you need a del.icio.us account. Accounts are free. Once you arrive at del.icio.us, look for the Sign Up Now area, and then create a username and supply your e-mail address.

Next, read the help page at del.icio.us to learn more about the service. It is located at http://del.icio.us/help/.

The most straightforward way to add a bookmark via del.icio.us is to click on the post link once you are logged in. You first supply a URL (I often copy and paste this in), and then you can provide a description and the tags. Use more than one tag by using spaces between them.

del.icio.us also provides a more convenient way to bookmark sites by using a browser button. This "button" is a piece of JavaScript, called a bookmarklet, that will take the URL of any site you are visiting and send that URL's data to your del.icio.us account. Once you have supplied your tags, del.icio.us will return you back to the Web site. The browser buttons may be found at http://del.icio.us/help/buttons/ and can be used with Firefox, Internet Explorer, Safari, and Opera.

Once you begin saving Web sites with del.icio.us, you can access your bookmark collection via RSS. The URL for this feed is http://del.icio.us/rss/*yourusername*. Unless bookmarks are marked private within del.icio.us, all bookmarks are published through this feed. Students should use caution when choosing a del.icio.us username—usernames should not include information that helps identify students, such as their birthday, real name, or zip code.

The first part of this lesson will include helping students set up del.icio.us accounts. As with many free Read/Write sites, they will need an e-mail address. The second part will include subscribing to their bookmarks via RSS. Conceivably, you could reverse this process—whereby an instructor first creates bookmarks for class use, and then students subscribe to the RSS feed using a desktop or Web-based aggregator.

Content area: Any subject area that lends itself to online research.

Synopsis: Students will use del.icio.us to bookmark research topics as part of an extended class in independent study. Teachers will monitor their research progress by subscribing to a del.icio.us RSS feed that tracks the students' bookmarks.

Standards: NETS•S: 2.d; 3.a, b, c; 5.c; 6.a

Age: Typically, independent research classes take place in the penultimate and ultimate years of a student's high school career.

Objectives: In conducting online research with a variety of online resources, students bookmark content using an account with del.icio.us. Students may also use Web site evaluation tools to rate the quality of content for each site, and use del.icio.us tags to apply ratings. Students will be assessed by the relevance and quality of their bookmarked sites in conjunction with their research topic.

Resources: Web browser, online search tools (including subscription-based research tools and/or general search engines), online video sources (such as Google Video, YouTube, etc.), podcasts, and a del.icio.us account

Procedure:
1. The instructor will work with students to establish a del.icio.us account. Students will report to the instructor the URL for the RSS feed associated with their account.

2. As students progress within the class (by conducting more and more online research), they use del.icio.us bookmarklets in their browser to tag and record potential resources for their research project.

3. Students will later review their bookmarks in del.icio.us by applying rating tags of their choosing and then adding notes to the bookmark. Examples might include "rating:5" as a tag for a good resource, or notes such as "helpful for how to identify chemical bonds."

4. Teachers will track student progress by subscribing to del.icio.us and the respective student-created RSS newsfeed.

Assessment: The research in an independent study course may play a major or minor role in the overall student assessment. In this lesson example, we could evaluate the student's online review of the resources they find based on the tags and notes used by the student when evaluating the quality of Web sites. Furthermore, if online evaluation checklists are used (such as Kathy Schrock's high school Web site evaluation checklist at http://school.discovery.com/ schrockguide/evalhigh.html), teachers may include the completion of these checklists as part of the evaluation.

Notes: This project can be expanded by asking students to use a blog to document their research project. Students can use the blog to journal their study, record Web sites, and even integrate the del.icio.us bookmarks into the blog. Plugins for the popular Word-Press blog engine exist to integrate one's del.icio.us account into the blog for easy, one-stop access. Beyond del.icio.us, a number of additional sites can be used to supply the social bookmarking service, including Furl (www.furl.net), Simpy (www.simpy.com), and Ma.gnolia (http://ma.gnolia.com). The Read Write Web site compares even more social bookmarking sites (www.readwriteWeb. com/archives/social_bookmarking_faceoff.php).

Lesson 4: *Photocasting*

Apple invented a new term with the release of their iLife '06 software suite. Within their iPhoto program, you can create and subscribe to "photocasts." The idea is clever: using their software and their subscription to ".Mac" services, you can publish your photos seamlessly with other iPhoto users. The technology behind photocasting? RSS! Photocasting support also enables us to subscribe to other RSS feeds that include photographs, even those not created with iPhoto.

In this lesson, we will use the popular online service Flickr to publish photos that students will use in multimedia projects. Since the distribution of high resolution photos can be problematic in many school labs, this solution leverages the power of a free, online service with RSS to provide a distribution medium of digital media. This setup can also facilitate your student photographers.

By creating a "group" in Flickr, you can invite other student photographers in your class or group to publish photos they take inside and outside of school. Everyone working in the classroom (or group) can then subscribe to the group's photo RSS feed. As an example, at NECC 2006 in San Diego, I joined a Flickr group. The URL for these photos is: www.flickr.com/groups/necc2006/pool/. Likewise, you can subscribe to this photocast via RSS—the feed link and buttons to add the feed to My Yahoo! and del.icio.us appear at the bottom of each Flickr page.

For Macintosh users who use iPhoto 6 (or later), this technique can also be leveraged using iPhoto and a (paid) ".Mac" account (instead of using Flickr). The feeds iPhoto creates can be subscribed to via Windows using a desktop aggregator, and iPhoto can be used to subscribe to non-iPhoto published feeds. In iPhoto 6, choose File > Subscribe to Photocast, and then paste-in a newsfeed that includes photos. iPhoto will download the latest 20 photos from Flickr newsfeeds.

When publishing photos to Flickr, take note of the ability to copyright and "tag" photos with keywords. Flickr leverages the Creative Commons licenses (http://creativecommons.org) within each user's settings. You can identify photos you upload as ones you are willing to share with others.

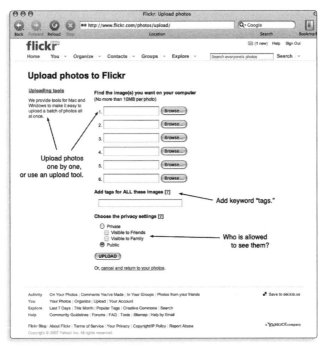

Figure 12.1 Start using Flickr.com by uploading photos and assigning tags.

Figure 12.2 Once your photos are online, look for the feed links at the bottom of your page. Now you are photocasting. Use these feeds in any news aggregator, or in a specialized program such as iPhoto.

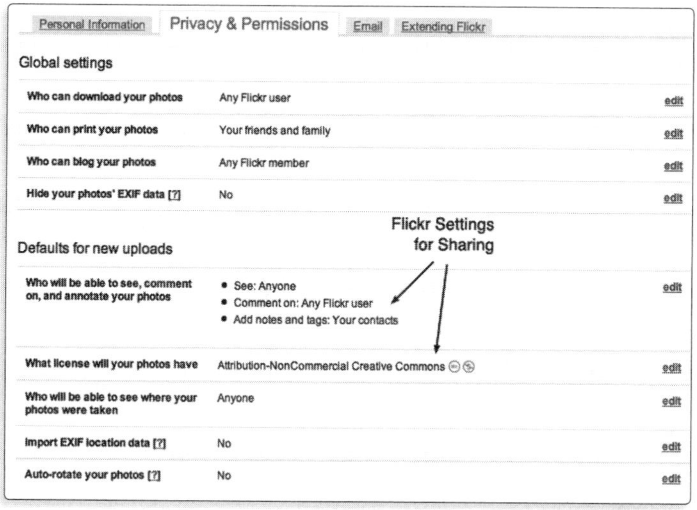

Figure 12.3 Visit Privacy and Permissions on your Flickr account to decide who can see the photos that are uploaded, and what licensing you automatically apply to new uploads.

Synopsis: Instructor and students will leverage the chore of managing photo media for a class project using Flickr and Flickr's RSS newsfeed. By photocasting their collective content, students will more easily be able to create a digital storytelling project using RSS.

Standards: NCTE: 4, 5, 6,8, 11

NETS•S: 1.b; 2.a, d; 3.b; 5.a

Age: Grades 4–12. Users of Flickr do a good job at self-moderating the photos used on the site. However, there will be photos that will be considered objectionable by some. I recommend resticting the uploading of photos to Flickr only to students who demonstrate the utmost responsibilty and maturity when using social services available to general public. All age levels can use the RSS newsfeed for obtaining photos from an instructor who is using Flickr to publish photos online.

Objectives: Students will construct a creative story based on a series of photographs. Students will transform their story into a multimedia experience using the photos combined with a reading of their story.

Digital storytelling is a wonderful activity to cover any number of content areas. For lesson ideas, consider the ideas online from the Western Massachusetts Writing Project: www.umass.edu/wmwp/ DigitalStorytelling/Lesson Plans for Digital Storytelling.htm.

This lesson example uses digital storytelling for a creative writing project. Students will consider a number of photos taken around their environment (which can include their school, their homes, and their community) as the impetus for a short story titled "Vacation in the Greatest Place." They will study the concept of *paradox* and use the details found in photographs to communicate why their mythical vacation place is ideal. Students consider questions relating to the photos: "Do pictures tell the whole story? Might pictures tell (or suggest) a different story altogether?" Students will use Flickr to manage the digital photos and then include the photos in their writing using a word processor. Students will use multimedia software to combine their photos and their writing in an engaging format. Lastly, students' writing will be considered as evidence of their understanding of paradox as a concept in literature and life.

Resources: digital camera, Flickr account(s), desktop or online news aggregator, word processor, digital movie software (e.g., Microsoft Movie Maker, Microsoft Photo Story, Audacity, Apple iMovie), storyboard planning sheet (many can be found online, including those from the Georgia Department of Education at: www.glc.k12. ga.us/trc/cluster.asp?mode=browse&intPathID=7801)

Procedure:

1. The instructor will introduce the concept of paradox, and students will be asked to identify examples of paradox from their experiences.

2. Students are asked, "Where might we take a vacation?" Student responses are likely to include familiar examples, such as the beach, a national park, a historic place, and so forth. Students are asked, "Could you take a vacation right here at home?"

3. Students consider photographs taken around their environment. Students may also participate by taking some photos around their home and community.

4. The instructor organizes photos using Flickr.com. Students subscribe to the Flickr RSS newsfeed with a news aggregator.

5. Students move photos from the aggregator to their computer and begin constructing a sequence of pictures.

6. Students write a short story on the topic "Vacation in the Greatest Place." The story should help market their community as an ideal vacation spot.

7. Students assemble their video using the digital photos and a recording of their story and then export the project as a movie/video file.

8. Students share the project with classmates, who may elect to evaluate the student's skill and creativity.

Assessment (60 points):

1. Did the student use good writing mechanics, including grammar, punctuation, and spelling in their story? (10 points)

2. Did the student's written story follow a logical progression of events, clearly identifying for the reader/listener why their vacation spot is ideal? (15 points)

3. Did the student use a storyboard to plan their writing, using digital photographs provided by the instructor/class? (10 points)

4. Using computer software, was the student successful in recording their written story into a digital format? (10 points)

5. Did the sequence of photos match the sequence in the story? (5 points)

6. Did the student's story show evidence of an understanding of paradox? (5 points)

7. Did the finished project show evidence of creativity? (5 points) This may be assessed by other classmates who have the opportunity to watch each storytelling project.

Notes: Many writing activities can follow this lesson, including reflections on other student projects. Projects will be more diverse when students are not required to use the same photos. However, when students *do* work from the same photos, they see different perspectives and learn to appreciate how others interpret the world.

As noted before, this lesson is but one strategy for using Flickr, RSS, and writing to facilitate a digital storytelling project. Photocasting can be used as a collection medium in a variety of scenarios, including the collection of data for scientific inquiry, the documentation of an event or performance, the documentation and authoring of personal histories, and for writing projects where a digital story (video) is not the ultimate product.

The projects completed in this lesson may be shared in the form of a videoblog or podcast to solicit comments from other students or the community.

Lesson 5: *Using Google Docs*

In the next couple of years, we will see more and more "desktop-quality" applications appear as online services. One of the most popular today is Google Docs (http://docs.google.com), which combines word processing and spreadsheet software into a Web-based application set. Beyond just a typical word processor and spreadsheet, however, Google's Apps allow for collaboration (so you can edit one document in tandem with another user in the same room, or across the world), the tracking of changes, multiple publication and output options (Word, PDF, export to blog), and—as we might have imagined—provides RSS support.

To use Google Docs, teachers and students need a Google account. Google has recently announced an education package for its Apps, which can provide a school the opportunity for their own domain name. You might consider this for providing students with the required e-mail access. Google Apps for Education (www.google.com/a/edu/) combines Gmail, Google Talk, Calendar, Docs, and their Page Creator—all under one online roof.

This example shows how you might use Google's services to subscribe to a student's personalized RSS feed and receive assignments. The lesson in this example introduces these products to students for the first time.

Content area: Any subject area where students are creating content or collecting data

Synopsis: Students will be encouraged to use Google Docs to hand-in assignments for use in several classes. Students will learn how to collaborate with fellow students and how to publish their work in a personalized, tag-word-specific newsfeed.

Standards: NETS•S: 2.a, 5.b, 6.b

Age: Grades 6–12

Objectives: Students will create a document using Google Docs, review rules in connection with using this service, and publish a custom RSS feed for the instructor to receive the document.

Resources: computer, Internet access, Google account, teacher account for online news aggregator

Procedure:

1. The instructor demonstrates RSS using an online news aggregator such as Google Reader.

2. Students review the school's Acceptable Use Policy (AUP) with regard to e-mail, plagiarism, network etiquette, and social responsibility. Students sign this AUP before receiving their Google Account credentials.

3. The instructor demonstrates the use of Google Docs—navigation and basic features.

4. Students review the Help documents to determine the differences between an owner, viewer, and collaborator in the Google Docs environment (http://docs.google.com/support/bin/answer.py?answer=50085).

5. Students create a new document that includes their name, e-mail address, and something they hope to

learn in the class. This may be augmented by answers to other questions the instructor wants to collect about students at the start of a school year or semester.

6. Students save and "Publish" the document.

7. Students view their documents (Browse Docs) after saving them, then click the check mark next to their new document.

8. From the Tag menu, students create a new tag for the document that identifies their class. This tag might be the subject area (e.g., Spanish) or the instructor's name.

9. Under Settings, students will look at their account settings and choose RSS Feeds.

10. Under the RSS feeds area, students will click on the feed link for the tag they just created (e.g., Spanish or the instructor's name).

11. Students confirm the feed link works, and they e-mail the new feed URL to their instructor.

12. The instructor now collects the class' documents and/or spreadsheets through this RSS feed. Students can create other tag/feed combinations for other instructors.

Assessment: Students can be assessed ultimately through the e-mail they send to teachers. Was an e-mail received? Did it include an RSS newsfeed link? Does the link work? Does the document students composed answer the questions posed to students? Have students signed and submitted the school's AUP in connection with using Google Docs?

Notes: The roles here can be reversed. Teachers can share their content via RSS with students by asking them to subscribe to their RSS feeds through Google Reader. Other Google services (such as their Calendar) also support RSS. This example obviously opens some risks with regard to cheating. The ability to share and collaborate openly with Google Apps obviously facilitates the sharing of content. If the classroom where this is implemented offers traditional assignments, such as book reports, essays, and quizzes, then Google Apps is probably not the appropriate tool. If, instead, the classroom is centered around project-based lessons where collaboration is encouraged, then students will enjoy having the ability to work together (through Google Talk, e-mail, and the sharing of documents), despite their physical location. Imagine laptops in a science lab where different portions of an experiment are taking place, and students can communicate about what is happening. The lab report can be filled out from disparate locations. An absent student could still participate from home.

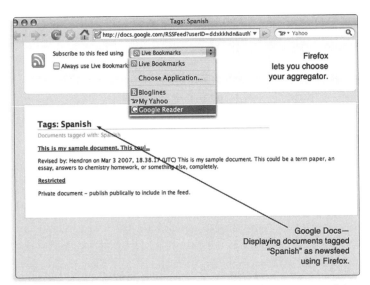

Figure 12.4 Google Docs' RSS in action: RSS feeds in the Firefox browser are called Live Bookmarks. You can subscribe to these within Firefox by bookmarking a Live bookmark, or you can choose your favorite aggregator from their drop-down menu.

RSS in this case, as it has been in others, is both a convenience and a productivity mechanism. Just as checking blogs via RSS is an easy way for the instructor to check up on student blogging, RSS is a great way to deliver notification that assignments are being handed-in.

CONCLUSION

The lessons included in this chapter reinforce Michael A. Looney's reality that "we live in a world filled with rich visuals and audio, communicated over many digital devices." RSS is a tool we can all use to harness content in a multiplicity of digital media.

CHAPTER **13**
Advanced RSS

Behind each of the technologies we have explored in ths book, RSS has played a role in making things work, from blogging and photocasting to keeping track of wikis.

I realize that working with content via RSS is not yet widespread. Beyond our students, consider how our students' parents operate on the Web. There are likely students you teach who have blogging parents. And, no doubt, there are other parents who don't know what a blog is. Some fathers have subscribed to RSS feeds on their handheld computers or smart phones. And some mothers listen to podcasts at the gym. Others, still, are exploring the Web for the first time. With such a diversified population, how do we help families leverage the content we and our students create?

RSS AND BACK AGAIN

One of the more interesting things you can do with an RSS feed is place its content back into an otherwise static Web page, creating an area of dynamic content. The following examples illustrate the convenience of RSS and its varied applications:

First, our county school district collected Web bookmarks using del.icio.us, and since the collection is social, anyone can see our links.

del.icio.us also augments each account with an RSS feed. Each time one of my colleagues adds a Web bookmark to our collection, the feed is updated. If you subscribe via RSS, you get an updated alert each time we update our collection of links. As we just postulated, however, not everyone participates online through RSS or Atom subscriptions. What we did, then, was to take our RSS list and plug it back into a Resources page on our Web site.

Second, when I redesigned our Web sites between 2004 and 2006, I designed new library media center pages for our librarians to maintain. When blogging came along, they had more than one page to keep updated. Their blogs were places to publish book reviews, news, and links for research. Their media center pages were more static, supplying research links, library hours, and QuickTime movies. It made sense, however, that all their content—the static links, permanent information, and their blog content—belonged together.

In the sidebar for each media center, I placed links to their blog post titles. These titles appear automatically, thanks to the RSS feed associated with their blogs. The process used to embed del.icio.us links and the blog feeds is a process that I refer to as disaggregation. It takes a newsfeed and parses the feed for the content, piece by piece, transforming it into a list of links.

This process is like RSS, but in reverse. It can also do some more profound things: Through the parsing of RSS feeds into your Web site, you can embed content from any source that uses RSS—news, blogs, and podcasts. With free tools found online, you can even mix your own customized RSS feed from disparate sources, creating a kind of "super feed" that takes content from disparate sources and re-displays it on your site the way you choose.

Why do this? Well, suppose you want to display all the blog posts from the 12 social studies teachers in your school under one area on your Web site. They could each be posting blog entries onto different blogs, using a mixture of blogging sites and blog platforms.

You first collect the newsfeed addresses, add them to a site that mixes feeds, and then take the super feed and process it for inclusion on your site. You have now created a single source to find all the content from your social studies department: blog posts, podcasts, and more; or a page that shows the world what your students are learning through their blog posts.

MIXING FEEDS

First, let us examine how to mix our own customized newsfeeds from various RSS sources. RSS Mix (www.rssmix.com) and Feed-Shake (www.feedshake.com) are two free services that combine disparate newsfeeds into a single new feed. Once you have established an account on one of the sites, copy-paste your newsfeed addresses into their site and generate a new feed. Your new customized feed can be displayed as a link on your Web site, appended to your e-mail signature, or used in the next process: parsing feeds.

PARSING FEEDS: USING DISAGGRAGATED RSS

There are a number of methods to take an aggrated feed and turn it back out into a Web page as a list, with the titles of the original newsfeeds each becoming a separate item. The first is to use MagpieRSS (http://magpierss.sourceforge.net). This is the more difficult solution to implement. Magpie is a news aggregator that works much like the others. It goes a step further by producing code that makes a list in HTML for your Web site. This is the tool I use to add our media specialist blog entries to their media center Web pages.

A more user-friendly tool that uses MagpieRSS is Feed2JS (http://feed2js.org). This free service essentially does the parsing on their server and provides JavaScript code for pasting into your blog or Web page. There are some advantages and disadvantages of using

JavaScript. The disadvantages are that some users disable JavaScript and some Web browsers may not present JavaScript data with the greatest accessibility.

The benefit of a solution like Feed2JS is the ease by which we can integrate a newsfeed into our Web site, without having to know anything about Server Side Includes (SSI), dynamic scripting, or the like. If you can copy and paste a few lines of code, you can use disaggregated RSS.

Feed Digest (www.feeddigest.com) and FeedBurner (www.feedburner.com) together provide some similar services for processing and re-using newsfeeds.

REFERENCES

Borja, R. (2005). Podcasting craze comes to K–12 schools. *Education Week, 25*(14) p. 8.

Bushweller, K. (2006). Thou shalt blog. *Teacher Magazine, 18*(3), p. 45.

Giles, J. (2005) Internet encyclopaedias go head to head. *Nature, 438,* 900–901. Available at www.nature.com/nature/journal/v438/n7070/full/438900a.html

Johnson, D. (n.d.) *Rules for pod people and a proposal for banning pencils.* The Blue Skunk Blog. Available at http://doug-johnson.squarespace.com/blue-skunk-blog/2005/9/28/rules-for-pod-people-and-a-proposal-for-banning-pencils.html

Kurzweil, R. (2005). *The singularity is near: When humans transcend biology.* New York: Viking Adult.

Looney, M. A. (2005). Giving students a 21st century education. *T.H.E. Journal, 33*(2), p. 58.

Marzano, R. J., Pickering, D., Pollock, J. E. (2004), *Classroom instruction that works: Research-based strategies for increasing student achievement.* Upper Saddle River, NJ: Prentice Hall.

McCloskey, P. J., (2006). The blogvangelist. *Teacher Magazine, 18*(2), p. 28.

Mid-continent Research for Education and Learning (McREL). (2003). Leadership folio series: Sustaining school improvement. Aurora, CO: Author.

New Oxford American Dictionary*, second edition.* (2005). New York: Oxford University Press.

Patrikakou, E. N. (2004). *Adolescence: Are parents relevant to students' high school achievement and post-secondary attainment?* Cambridge, MA: Harvard Family Research Project, Harvard University. Available at http://www.gse.harvard.edu/hfrp/projects/fine/ resources/digest/adolescence.html

Tapscott, D. & Williams, A. D. (2006). *Wikinomics: How mass collaboration changes everything.* New York: Portfolio Hardcover.

Weiss, H., Kreider, H., Levine, E., Mayer, E., Stadler, J., and Vaughan, P. (1998). *Beyond the parent–teacher conference: Diverse patterns of home–school communication.* Paper presented at the American Educational Research Association Annual Conference, San Diego, CA. Available at www.gse.harvard.edu/hfrp/pubs/onlinepubs/beyondptc.html

SCREENSHOT/ARTWORK CREDITS

Cover artwork
Artwork © istockphoto.com/centauria
RSS icon © istockphoto.com/Bibigon

Chapter 5
iTunes screenshots © Apple Inc.
FeedForAll screenshots © NotePage, Inc.

Chapter 7
Audacity screenshots are © 2007 members of the
Audacity development team.

Chapter 8
GarageBand sceenshots © Apple Inc.

Chapter 9
WordPress screenshots © WordPress.
ecto screenshots © ecto/Alex Hung.

Chapter 10
NetNewsWire screenshots © NewsGator Technologies, Inc.
Google Reader screenshots © Google.

Chapter 11
Internet Explorer screenshots © Microsoft Corporation.

Chapter 13
Flickr screenshots © Yahoo! Inc.
Google Docs screenshots © Google.

Web Resources for RSS, Podcasting, and Social Computing

The following Web sites and URLs make up my emerging and growing catalog of services and resources for RSS, podcasting, and instances of social computing. Many of the links listed here appear within the previous pages, but not all. Some are too new and beyond the scope of this book. While the list is long, it is not exhaustive. My aim is to provide a comprehensive list of best-in-class examples of the current state of the Read/Write Web. I hope you will find these useful. They will likely jump-start new ideas and more interesting endeavors.

My guiding principle as an instructional technologist has always been to empower teachers with technology. Of course, it is the students who benefit most from using great technology; yet, I feel that teachers need to have a comfort with technology—they need to "own" it, not only for their professional endeavors, but to acquire 21st century competency. Adopting Read/Write skills in your daily life will undoubtedly change your perception of the world and influence your pedagogy. When teachers believe in these tools, a classroom can be truly transformed, reaping the benefits that Read/Write technologies offer in the form of creativity, collaboration, and communication.

I wish you—the teacher, the administrator, and the technology coordinator—the best of luck in adopting these tools for use with your students and in your schools. Read/Write tools will likely only get more sophisticated, easier to use, and more prevalent in our future culture. The recipe for success includes a pinch of dare and adventure, with ample amounts of high-bandwidth access and plenty of computers. I encourage you to remember that learning can be fun, and to look for fun and exciting ways to implement blogs, wikis, podcasts, and synchronous communications in your classroom.

TITLE	URL	DESCRIPTION
$100 Laptop project	http://laptop.org	Home to the $100 Laptop Project that is focused on providing an educational laptop to students around the world, with a focus on developing nations.
23 Photo Sharing	www.23hq.com	Free photo sharing; similar to Flickr.
43 Things	www.43things.com	Social Web site where folks establish life goals; includes RSS newsfeed.
Apple iTunes	www.apple.com	Popular music jukebox player for Macs and PCs; includes podcast support and a podcast directory.
Apple Podcasting Server	www.apple.com/ education/solutions/ podcasting/server.html	Mac OS X Tiger Server (software; requires Apple hardware) includes a blogging and podcasting server that's easy to use.
Ask Metafilter	http://ask.metafilter.com	Community-based blog where visitors ask questions; other members post responses and vote on the best responses.

TITLE	URL	DESCRIPTION
Audacity	http://audacity. sourceforge.net	Open-source audio editor for Windows, Linux, and Macintosh.
Bebo	www.bebo.com	Social networking site, popular with teens.
Blogbeat	www.blogbeat.net	Statistics about your blog visitors.
Blogger	www.blogger.com	Free blog service.
BlogJet	http://blogjet.com	Windows-based blog editor.
Bloglines	www.bloglines.com	Online news aggregator.
BlogSieve	www.blogsieve.com	Creates new RSS feeds by combining/filtering others.
Box	www.box.net	Free and pay-online storage accounts. A place to put files and backups, with RSS support for sharing.
CalendarHub	http://calendarhub.com	Web-based calendars for sharing, complete with RSS.
California Open Source Textbook Project	www.opensourcetext.org	A place to work on and share open-source textbooks.
Camtasia Studio for Windows	www.techsmith.com	Makes screen shots and movies of your computer's display.
Center for Media Literacy	www.medialit.org	Resources for teaching media literacy skills to students.

TITLE	URL	DESCRIPTION
Community Server	http://communityserver.org	Windows IIS-based blogging platform.
Creative Commons	http://creativecommons.org	Support for sharing creative work with deeds that encourage sharing and "prosumerism."
del.icio.us	http://del.icio.us/	Social bookmarking; Web favorites get tagged with keywords.
Digg	http://digg.com	Digg invites users to vote for online content, creating "best of the best" lists for browsing.
Digital Future Project	www.digitalcenter.org	Information source for Internet-related trends.
Discussion App	http://server.com/ communityapps/ discussionapp/	For creating discussion groups with RSS feeds.
Drupal	http://drupal.org	Open-source content management system with blogs.
ecto	http://ecto.kung-foo.tv	Windows- and Mac-based blog editor.
EduBlogs	http://edublogs.org	Free blogs for educators and students.
Education Podcast Network	www.epnWeb.org	Directory of education-related podcasts; grouped in categories.
Edupodder	www.edupodder.com	Blog and podcast about podcasting in education.
Electronic Frontier Foundation	www.eff.org	Organization poised on netizen rights, examining issues with copyright.

TITLE	URL	DESCRIPTION
Expression Engine	http://expressionengine.com	Blog and content management system that runs on your server.
Facebook	www.facebook.com	Popular social networking site originally for college students.
Favoor	www.favoor.com	Start page for the Web with RSS aggregation feature.
Feed2JS	http://jade.mcli.dist.maricopa.edu/feed/	Turns RSS newsfeeds into JavaScript for inclusion within your Web site.
FeedBurner	www.feedburner.com	Takes blogs and simple RSS newsfeeds and creates newsfeeds; can be used with a Blogger.com account to add support for podcasts.
Feed Digest	www.feeddigest.com	Turns RSS newsfeeds into code that can be included into your Web site.
Feeder— Reinvented Software	www.reinventedsoftware.com/feeder/	Creates RSS newsfeeds, including podcast feeds, for Mac OS X.
FeedForAll	www.feedforall.com	Desktop application for creating RSS newsfeeds; Windows and Mac versions available.
FeedShake	www.feedshake.com	Manages multiple newsfeeds by merging and sorting.
FeedSpring	www.usablelabs.com/feedspring.html	Creates RSS newsfeeds, including podcast feeds, for Windows.
Feedster	www.feedster.com	Search engine for RSS newsfeeds.

TITLE	URL	DESCRIPTION
FireAnt	http://fireant.tv	Find video podcasts.
Flickr	www.flickr.com	Photo sharing Web site; can photocast pictures via RSS.
Freeplay Music	www.freeplaymusic.com	Source for music for use in podcast productions; you must now license music from Freeplay to legally use it; educational discounts apply.
Fruitcast	www.fruitcast.com	Web service for earning cash through your podcast with advertising.
FURL	www.furl.net	Another social bookmarking tool.
Gada	www.gada.be	Meta-search engine that can supply results in RSS.
GarageBand	www.apple.com/ilife/garageband/	A music-production and podcast-creation tool for Mac OS X.
Gizmo Call	www.gizmocall.com	Gizmo VoIP service through a Web page.
Gizmo Project	www.gizmoproject.com	VoIP service for phone-to-computer and computer-to-computer calls.
Gliffy	www.gliffy.com	Make charts and diagrams through the Web.
Google Blog Search	http://blogsearch.google.com	Leading blog search engine.

TITLE	URL	DESCRIPTION
Google Docs	http://docs.google.com	Google Apps are Web-based and invite collaboration through sharing. Applications currently offered are word processor, calendar, spreadsheet, and e-mail.
Google News	http://news.google.com	News and RSS newsfeeds of Google news.
Google Reader	www.google.com/reader	Online news aggregator.
GreatNews	www.curiostudio.com	Windows-based RSS aggregator.
Instiki	www.instiki.org	The instant wiki; uses the Ruby scripting language with its own embedded Web server.
iPodder.org	www.ipodder.org/directory/4/podcasts/categories/educational/	Podcasting directory of educational podcasts.
iShowU	http://shinywhitebox.com/home/home.html	Application for taking screen movies on Mac OS X.
JotSpot	www.jot.com	Wiki hosting.
Learning in Hand	www.learninginhand.com	Free podcasting templates.
LibriVox	www.librivox.org	Free public domain texts in audio format.
Libsyn Pro	http://libsynpro.com	Service for uploading, hosting, and creating podcasts.
Live Journal	www.livejournal.com	Popular blogging portal.

TITLE	URL	DESCRIPTION
localendar	www.rsscalendar.com/rss/	Create a calendar with RSS support; also includes data based on your location.
Lyceum	http://lyceum.ibiblio.org	Open-source implementation of WordPress for multiple blogs.
Ma.gnolia Social Bookmarking	http://ma.gnolia.com	Find and save Web bookmarks.
MagpieRSS	http://magpierss. sourceforge.net	Turns RSS newsfeeds back into HTML for inclusion within your Web site.
MarsEdit	www.red-sweater.com/ marsedit/	Mac-based blog editor.
Measure Map	www.measuremap.com	Statistics about your blog visitors.
MediaWiki	www.mediawiki.org	Open-source wiki engine that powers Wikipedia.
Metafilter	www.metafilter.com	Community-based blog where users share what is of interest online and beyond.
MIT Open-CourseWare	http://ocw.mit.edu	Free college course materials available to the public.
Moodle	http://moodle.org	An open-source course management system.
Movable Type	www.movabletype.com	Extensible pay-for blogging platform; supports multiple blogs.
MySpace	www.myspace.com	Hugely popular community and social network.

TITLE	URL	DESCRIPTION
NetNewsWire / NetNews-Wire Lite	http://ranchero.com/netnewswire/	News-aggregator application for Mac OS X.
NewsGator	www.newsgator.com	Desktop and online news aggregators for Macs and PCs.
Newsvine	www.newsvine.com	Find breaking stories through RSS.
Odeo	www.odeo.com	Free, online podcast creation and aggregation service.
Open Source CMS	www.opensourcecms.com	Site for evaluating open-source content management systems.
Opera Browser	www.opera.com	Multi-platform, standards-compliant browser with RSS support.
Partnership for 21st Century Skills	www.21stcentury-skills.org	Site identifies work skills likely required in a future society.
PBwiki	http://pbwiki.com	Free site for setting up your own wiki. Paid plans are available for users who need more space.
Performancing Plugin	http://performancing.com/firefox	Blog editor that works with Firefox.
PmWiki	www.pmwiki.org	Wiki engine that stores wiki content in flat files, instead of a database. Supports wiki groups, each with their own control via passwords for read, write, and upload.
Podcast Free America	http://podcastfreeamerica.com	Podcasting advice.

TITLE	URL	DESCRIPTION
Podcast Monkey	www.softwaresinge.com/ site/content/ blogcategory/23/43/	Mac OS X tool for creating RSS newsfeeds.
Podcast.net	www.podcast.net	Podcast directory.
Podscope	http://podscope.com	Search engine for finding video and audio content from podcasts.
Podzinger	www.podzinger.com	Podcast directory.
Remember the Milk	www.rememberthemilk.com	To-Do list manager.
Reminder-Feed	www.reminderfeed.com	Keep track of life events via RSS.
RMail	www.r-mail.org	Send RSS newsfeeds to your e-mail inbox.
RSS 2 PDF	http://rss2pdf.com	Converts RSS newsfeeds to PDF documents.
RSS Calendar	www.rsscalendar.com/rss/	Create an RSS-enabled calendar to share.
RSS Mix	www.rssmix.com	Create "super feeds" by combining multiple RSS feeds into a single feed.
RssReader	www.rssreader.com	News-aggregator application for Windows.
Second Life	http://secondlife.com	The Linden Lab 3D environment for social networking and business opportunities.
SharpReader	www.sharpreader.net	News-aggregator application for Windows.

TITLE	URL	DESCRIPTION
Shoutwire	www.shoutwire.com	Internet news—hot news stories delivered via RSS.
Simply Hired	www.simplyhired.com	Job search engine; results can be delivered via RSS.
Simpy	www.simpy.com	Social bookmark service.
Skype	www.skype.com	VoIP service for phone-to-computer and computer-to-computer calls.
SnapzProX for Mac OS X	www.ambrosiasw.com	Makes screen shots and movies of your computer's display.
Soundtrack Pro	www.apple.com/finalcutstudio/soundtrackpro/	Pro-level sound/podcast editor for Mac OS X.
Squeet	www.squeet.com	Turns your e-mail account into an RSS newsreader.
Straw	www.gnome.org/projects/straw/	News-aggregator application for the GNOME desktop environment (Linux).
SubEthaEdit	www.codingmonkeys.de	A unique-in-class text editor for Macintosh that allows collaboration across both local- and wide-area networks. Students in one classroom will see one another immediately when the application is launched, and they can share and join other documents being hosted on one another's computer.
SuprGlu	www.suprglu.com	Gathers content from various Web 2.0 services into one page for easy management (bookmarks, blogs, etc.).

TITLE	URL	DESCRIPTION
Syndic8	www.syndic8.com	Finds newsfeeds.
Ta-da Lists	www.tadalist.com	Web 2.0 service that helps you establish To-Do lists.
Talkr	www.talkr.com	Converts text-based blogs into audioblogs—creates podcasts.
Teachers' TV Podcast	www.teachers.tv/podcasting	Education content in video; plays back on iPod with video.
Technorati	www.technorati.com	Leading blog search engine.
Textpattern	www.textpattern.com	Free content management system for blogging. This can be installed on your own server, or through a web hosting package. An alternative to WordPress.
TypePad	www.typepad.com	Easy-to-use pay-for blogging service.
Upcoming	http://upcoming.org	Social event calendar with syndication to blogs.
Vaestro	www.vaestro.com	Free service for integrating voice comments into Web sites and blogs.
Vox	www.vox.com	Community-centered blogging portal.
w.bloggar	http://wbloggar.com	Windows-based blog editor.
Wikipedia	http://en.wikipedia.org	Free, online encyclopedia based around the wiki concept; with entries in multiple languages.

TITLE	URL	DESCRIPTION
Wikispaces	www.wikispaces.com	Free and paid accounts for wikis.
WordPress	http://wordpress.org	Free weblog platform; gets installed on your own server; includes RSS support for podcasts.
WordPress MU	http://mu.wordpress.org	Multiple-user version of Word-Press; this software powers EduBlogs and WordPress.com.
Writeboard	www.writeboard.com	Virtual whiteboard/wiki that can be shared and subscribed to via RSS.
Yahoo! 360°	http://360.yahoo.com	News aggregator, start-page, blog—all rolled into one.
Yahoo! News	http://news.yahoo.com	News and RSS newsfeeds of news from Yahoo!
Yahoo! Podcasts	http://podcasts.yahoo.com	Podcast directory.
YouTube	www.youtube.com	Site for sharing and watching video clips.

Glossary

Terms used throughout the book are organized here by chapter.

INTRODUCTION

Atom
: Atom is an alternative, competing format to RSS. Most all news aggregators understand Atom as well as the various versions of RSS.

audioblogs
: Blogs that use audio content as the posting medium. If the audioblog supports syndication, the blog becomes a platform for publishing audio podcasts.

blogosphere
: A term describing blog-generated content on the Web that is linked together with blogrolls, trackbacks, and permalinks.

blogroll
: A list of favorite blogs or Web sites, often found on a blog. It's a way of saying to a reader: "If you like what I write, you may also like these authors."

Creative Commons
: A set of "deeds" content creators can apply to their works that lessen the restrictions of traditional copy-right. By applying a Creative Commons license to your work, you declare you are willing to share the content with others. A variety of licenses are available to choose from.

cyberspace	A term describing content found over the Internet, as if the Web or Internet occupied an actual physical space. *Cyberspace* is often interchangeable with *Internet*.
hacking	A term that today refers to nondestructive tinkering and modification of something. (Compare the term with "cracking," which refers to elicit behavior with a negative connotation.) Hacking is at the core of the so-called prosumer revolution.
HTML	Hypertext Markup Language. The markup language used to format content and set up hypertext links on the Web.
iPod	Currently the market leader for MP3 players. Apple's iconic device also carries your calendar, addresses, phone numbers, and games; can be used with a variety of accessories, including microphones to record content.
iTunes	Apple's digital jukebox program for Macs and PCs. iTunes manages music on your computer; also manages content that is transferred to iPods, including movies, pictures, and, of course, music.
news aggregator	A browser for newsfeeds. Aggregators can be a type of Web site (Bloglines, Google Reader), a desktop application (Sharp Reader, NetNewsWire), or simply embedded within other applications (iTunes or Internet Explorer).
newsfeed	A generic term referring to the XML file that holds data in individual chunks. We might call each chunk a "news story." Each story has a title and metadata—information about where the story comes from (e.g., your Web site), and when it was published. The RSS or Atom file on a Web server is the newsfeed.

permalink

A Web link that points to a specific blog post. Because blog posts move around as new posts are made, permalinks enable linking to a specific post (instead of just to the blog's general Web site).

podcasts

Multimedia files (audio and video) that are distributed via RSS. Podcasting has been identified as a new era of broadcasting, where anyone with access to the Internet can easily publish and distribute "shows" modeled after TV and radio.

Read/Write Web

This term refers to the new era of the World Wide Web, where computer users are not just passively searching for information, but are contributing to the content themselves. This term is sometimes used to describe "Web 2.0." This new Web is facilitated through new tools that make publishing content easy.

Really Simple Syndication (RSS)

RSS refers to both a standard and a technology used to deliver online content. RSS 2.0 is a specific standard. RSS 2.0 is a file written in XML that includes support for attachments, such as JPEG pictures and MP3 sound files. When referred to as a technology, it may also include a second syndication standard called Atom. Both Atom and RSS links are found on today's Web sites. They both work with a class of application called a news aggregator. Looking at the RSS file, news aggregators collect new content that is automatically published to a site at regular intervals.

Second Life

An online, three-dimensional world that mimics a video game. Instead of a game, however, Second Life invites its "citizens" to create their own world and encourages business through Second Life's currency system.

Tim Berners-Lee

The creator of the World Wide Web and the HTML language used to format Web pages. Berners-Lee's original vision for the Web included easy editing of content through a desktop-based editor.

trackback	Similar to a permalink, a trackback link connects your new blog post to the blog post of another author on another blog. The cool thing that happens is that a link to your blog post appears on the original poster's blog. Trackbacks connect blogs together on a by-post basis, forming a "web" of content. You can also think of trackbacks as blog comments that are posts on other blogs.
videoblogs	Blogs that use video content as the posting medium. If the videoblog supports syndication, a videoblog can be a publishing platform for video podcasts.
Web 2.0	This term has a number of interpretations. It refers to a new class of Web sites that have desktop-application-like functionality, with some using a set of Web-development technologies called AJAX. The term also refers to our new era of Read/Write Web sophistication, where anyone can contribute through a variety of media, including blogs, podcasts, wikis, and social Web sites (where online communities are flourishing around common interests and functions).
webcasts	Audio and video content that is streamed over the Internet in real-time. Some Webcasts are live events. Instead of receiving a file, you watch a webcast on the computer like live television.
weblogs	Weblogs, or blogs, are a style of Web site that emerged in the second-half of the 1990s. Organized around short posts of information, some resemble online diaries; others point to other content of interest on the Web, with commentary from the blog's author(s). Blogs typically use a database to store content, and use an "engine" or "platform" to dynamically organize the content on the Web in reverse-chronological order (with the most recent posts at the top).
wikis	Web pages that can be edited on-screen, within a browser. Many use some form of "wikitext" (wiki markup language) for creating links and styling text.

XML	Extensible Markup Language. A tagging language, like HTML, that organizes data. Newsfeed files are formatted with XML. Much like with HTML files, you can edit XML files in a text editor.

CHAPTER 1

metadata	Information about additional data (data about data). When you take a digital photograph, your camera stores metadata (information about the photo) with the JPEG file. This is how your computer knows when it was taken and what camera settings were used. Blog posts use metadata to record who wrote the post, when it was authored, and what categories or tags apply to the post.

CHAPTER 2

Bonjour	First called Rendezvous, Apple, Inc.'s implementation of the open-source networking protocol called Zeroconf (Zero Configuration Networking). It allows for easy setup of printers on a network. Devices "auto discover" themselves. Used with iChat A/V software, you can instantly discover other iChat users on your local network's buddy list, without having to manually add them. Other software services announce themselves on the network, including photo sharing, music sharing, and Web sharing.
Markdown	A formatting language used to mark-up text in blogs, wikis, and other content management systems. http://daringfireball.net/projects/markdown/
Textile	A formatting language used to mark-up text in blogs, wikis, and other content management systems. www.textism.com/tools/textile/
Wikitext	A formatting language used to mark-up text on a wiki. Wikitext is used in lieu of more complex formatting technologies, such as HTML or CSS (Cascading Style Sheets).

WikiWikiWeb

The original wiki. It first appeared at: http://c2.com. The concept of online, in-browser editing has caught on. A variety of server-side applications now support wiki editing.

CHAPTER 3

burning

A term describing the writing of data to an optical disc, such as a CD-R or DVD-R disc. "Burning a CD" means copying data onto a CD. You can only write (burn) to discs with an "-R" (Record) or "-R/W" (Record/Write) designation.

content management system (CMS)

Server software that manages content, including text, audio, and video. Blogs are a class of CMS. Most use a template system to control the look of content online, and a database (SQL) to store the content.

FLV

Flash video. A popular video format requiring the use of Adobe's Flash plugin (formerly Macromedia Flash). Since so many computers today have Flash already installed, it's used to circumvent instances where other formats may be unavailable on a user's machine (e.g., Real, QuickTime, Windows Media).

FTP

File Transfer Protocol. Software and protocol used to transfer files between clients and servers. You are encouraged to use a modern variant, called SFTP (secure FTP). It is a safer way to transfer content from your computer and a Web server.

LAME

"Lame Ain't an MP3 Encoder"—strange name, for sure; a free compression engine for creating top-quality MP3 recordings available for Windows, Macs, and Linux. You must install LAME independently of Audacity to create MP3 files from within Audacity.

MP3   MP3 is a common compressed audio format that can be created and played on a variety of equipment, without regard to platform or digital rights management restrictions. MP3 is the most universal audio format and a good choice for audio podcast productions.

CHAPTER 4

avatar   A small icon or picture used to identify users in online communities. The avatar could be a small photograph or graphic, or an artistic drawing or character from a movie or television show. Discussion boards and some blogs include your avatar each time you make a contribution.

communal constructivism   Expanding upon social constructivist thought, this learning theory supports students creating the means through which learning takes place. See: https://www.cs.tcd.ie/publications/tech-reports/reports.01/TCD-CS-2001–04.pdf

CompactFlash   Another portable storage format used in digital cameras, voice recorders, and other devices. CompactFlash is popular in high-end digital cameras.

FireWire   A high-speed serial connection, also referred to as IEEE-1394. FireWire has a maximum speed of 400 Mbits/second, which is used for high-speed applications (external CD burners, hard drives, digital video). FireWire 800 is a newer format, with a maximum speed of 800 Mbits/second.

Flash   A software application and file format. Adobe Flash (formerly Macromedia Flash) lets authors animate content and produce interactive movies. Flash (.swf) files are popular as multimedia content embedded within Web pages. The Flash plugin is required to see/hear this content (see also *FLV*, chapter 5).

Google Talk
: Google's implementation of instant messaging, in competition with AOL's Instant Messenger (AIM), Microsoft's Network Messenger (MSN Messenger), and newcomers like Skype. Google Talk works over the Jabber protocol.

high-speed USB
: Also called USB 2, high-speed USB is used on iPods and hard drives and has a maximum speed of 480 Mbits/second. Traditionally, USB has been favored on Windows-based PCs; whereas, FireWire has been more popular on Macs.

Jabber
: An open-source protocol for providing chat services. By running your own Jabber server, you can restrict users to communicating only with other users on that server. Jabber could be used, for instance, to enable school-based instant messaging for students and teachers in a closed system.

SD card
: A secure digital (SD) card is a portable storage format used in digital cameras, PDAs, and other devices. SD cards are usually quite small (generally, 32 mm x 24 mm x 2.1 mm thick).

social constructivism
: A philosophical theory that people learn from creating their own knowledge, born from the social interactions they have with others. This learning theory supports project-based learning.

texting
: Text-messaging. Sometimes referred to as SMS (short message service). SMS messages can be sent between cellular phones, personal digital assistants (PDAs), and computers.

USB
: Universal Serial Bus (USB) is the serial mechanism on modern computers for connecting mice, keyboards, scanners, and hard drives. The "bus" refers to the physical connections that route the port (where you plug a cord in) to the computer's processor. When many devices share one bus or signal path, performance can suffer. (Compare, if you will, a bus with many devices to a busy highway.)

USB flash drive	Sometimes called a "thumb" or "stick" drive, this device holds data on flash-ROM chips in capacities from 128 MB to beyond 4 GB.
WAV	Sometimes written as "WAVE," this is the default sound format on Windows. WAV files can be full CD-quality (16-bit, 44.1 kHz) or compressed. Many voice recorders, including the iPod, record in WAV format.

CHAPTER 5

AIFF	Audio Interchange File Format. The file format for CD-audio. Like some WAV files, AIFF files are typically 16-bit, 44.1kHz. MP3 files are generally 10-times smaller than full-quality AIFF files.
bitrate	A measure of how much data is recorded in each sample within a compressed file. The maximum bitrate for MP3 is 320 kbits/second. Many folks cannot distinguish the difference between an original source recording with MP3 at 160 kbits/second. At bitrates less than 96 for stereo recordings, sound recordings gain a "crunchy" sound. The quality of your source recording and your desired file size for compressed audio and video files will determine which bitrate offers a compromise between quality and file size.
codecs	Standing for compress-decompress, a codec is a software algorithm for treating audio and video to produce smaller files. JPEG, GIF, MP3, AAC, WMA are all codecs. "Lossy" codecs throw away information to compress files, so they transfer more quickly over a network. FLAC (Free Lossless Audio Codec) is an example of a lossless codec for audio, which reproduces the original content yet saves about half the file size. Popular media players, including Windows Media Player and QuickTime, use different codecs to process and play back media files. Some codecs are open (MP3), meaning the content is easily copied. Other codecs are closed and contain DRM (digital rights management) software, whereby copies cannot be made.

compression
Compression is a process where a digital file is manipulated to save file space, which yields faster transfers over a network. So-called lossy compression in audio files removes details the human ear has difficulty hearing, and averages out fine details. Files are compressed using a codec.

enhanced podcasts
Apple's term for an audio podcast that contains embedded pictures. Apple's GarageBand software makes enhanced podcasts by embedding JPEG files within a file with MPEG-4 compressed audio. The file extension for enhanced podcasts is .m4a (mpeg-4 audio). Enhanced podcasts can be made with other codecs, too, but are not currently as popular as M4A files.

interstitials
Sometimes called bumpers, these are transitional audio clips that are inserted between scenes in a podcast production. Likewise, you can have video interstitials in video productions, dividing scenes with smaller content chunks.

monaural
Original sound recordings were made with a single audio source. "Mono" recordings include only one of the two stereo channels. Converting a stereo recording to mono cuts the file size in half; however, monaural recordings lose their depth of sound and their inherent sense of three-dimensional space.

open-source
Often interchangeable with *free*, open-source software is licensed with source code, where programmers have teamed-up to write the software together. Successful open-source projects include MySQL, the database software; Apache, the Web server; and PHP, a scripting language. Typically, open-source software is free to install and use on your computer, but it comes with no warrantees or guarantees. Support for open-source software is typically delivered through discussion boards and online user communities. The price of open-source software is attractive to publicly funded entities such as schools.

shuttle controls	Buttons for controlling playback in an audio or video editor. These resemble the control buttons on a VCR or tape deck and include record, reverse, stop, pause, play, and fast-forward.
waveforms	Graphical representations of audio clips.

CHAPTER 6

AAC	Advanced Audio Coding is an MPEG-4-based audio codec used in content sold by Apple (through iTunes). AAC has two variants—an open one and a digital-rights-management feature that restricts who can playback the files.
feedback loop	A cycle that is formed when the microphone is too close to the audio speaker(s). The audio builds up and becomes more and more distorted. Typically, this is a loud, undesired effect in audio recording.
.m4a	The file extension used by QuickTime for enhanced podcasts. .m4v is used for MPEG-4-encoded video for use on the iPod.
MPEG-4	A new generation of audio codecs used for compressing audio and video, developed as an open standard by the Motion Picture Experts Group (MPEG).
QuickTime	From Apple, Inc., QuickTime is a playback system for Macs and PCs. QuickTime uses both open- and proprietary codecs for compressing audio and video. Podcasts available through iTunes are all QuickTime-compatible.

CHAPTER 7

intranet	An internal network of services. Schools and corporations maintain intranets to provide Web-like services (file sharing, Web pages, etc.) to a closed group (e.g., students and employees), typically behind a firewall.

smart phones	A class of cell phones that offer Internet connectivity, e-mail, and other features found in more traditional personal desktop assistants (PDAs).
timestamp	Metadata that records the date and time of creation. Timestamps are applied to blog comments and posts to show when they were authored.
XML-RPC	XML remote procedure call. For blogging, a method by which another application can communicate with the blogging software on a server. This enables applications like ecto to let you author blog posts on your desktop computer. Most modern blog software contains support for remote editing and publishing via XML-RPC.

CHAPTER 8

XML badges	Typically orange, XML badges identify RSS or Atom newsfeed files on Web sites.

CHAPTER 9

handle	An alias, or online identity. Handles refer to your alias in chat rooms, online communities, and in discussion boards.
tagging	The act of applying keywords or "tags" to online content. Tagging has been proposed as a modern method for organizing an overload of content. Tags can help filter information in future searches.

CHAPTER 12

bookmarklet	A link you place in your browser that does more than just load a Web page. Bookmarklets contain JavaScript code that performs a useful task; for example, the bookmarklet used with del.icio.us identifies the site you are on and your login credentials, so you can easily update your del.icio.us list with a one-click "button."

National Educational Technology Standards

National Educational Technology Standards for Students (NETS•S)

The National Educational Technology Standards for students are divided into six broad categories. Standards within each category are to be introduced, reinforced, and mastered by students. Teachers can use these standards as guidelines for planning technology-based activities in which students achieve success in learning, communication, and life skills.

1. Creativity and Innovation

Students demonstrate creative thinking, construct knowledge, and develop innovative products and processes using technology. Students:

- a. apply existing knowledge to generate new ideas, products, or processes.

- b. create original works as a means of personal or group expression.

- c. use models and simulations to explore complex systems and issues.

- d. identify trends and forecast possibilities.

2. Communication and Collaboration

Students use digital media and environments to communicate and work collaboratively, including at a distance, to support individual learning and contribute to the learning of others Students:

  a. interact, collaborate, and publish with peers, experts, or others employing a variety of digital environments and media.

  b. communicate information and ideas effectively to multiple audiences using a variety of media and formats.

  c. develop cultural understanding and global awareness by engaging with learners of other cultures.

  d. contribute to project teams to produce original works or solve problems.

3. Research and Information Fluency

Students apply digital tools to gather, evaluate, and use information. Students:

  a. plan strategies to guide inquiry.

  b. locate, organize, analyze, evaluate, synthesize, and ethically use information from a variety of sources and media.

  c. evaluate and select information sources and digital tools based on the appropriateness to specific tasks.

  d. process data and report results.

4. Critical Thinking, Problem Solving, and Decision Making

Students use critical-thinking skills to plan and conduct research, manage projects, solve problems, and make informed decisions using appropriate digital tools and resources.

Students:

a. identify and define authentic problems and significant questions for investigation.

b. plan and manage activities to develop a solution or complete a project.

c. collect and analyze data to identify solutions and make informed decisions.

d. use multiple processes and diverse perspectives to explore alternative solutions.

5. Digital Citizenship

Students understand human, cultural, and societal issues related to technology and practice legal and ethical behavior. Students:

a. advocate and practice the safe, legal, and responsible use of information and technology.

b. exhibit a positive attitude toward using technology that supports collaboration, learning, and productivity.

c. demonstrate personal responsibility for lifelong learning.

d. exhibit leadership for digital citizenship.

6. Technology Operations and Concepts

Students demonstrate a sound understanding of technology concepts, systems, and operations. Students:

a. understand and use technology systems.

b. select and use applications effectively and productively.

c. troubleshoot systems and applications.

d. transfer current knowledge to the learning of new technologies.

National Educational Technology Standards for Teachers (NETS•T)

All classroom teachers should be prepared to meet the following standards and performance indicators.

I. Technology Operations and Concepts

Teachers demonstrate a sound understanding of technology operations and concepts. Teachers:

    A. demonstrate introductory knowledge, skills, and understanding of concepts related to technology (as described in the ISTE NETS•S).

    B. demonstrate continual growth in technology knowledge and skills to stay abreast of current and emerging technologies.

II. Planning and Designing Learning Environments and Experiences

Teachers plan and design effective learning environments and experiences supported by technology. Teachers:

    A. design developmentally appropriate learning opportunities that apply technology-enhanced instructional strategies to support the diverse needs of learners.

    B. apply current research on teaching and learning with technology when planning learning environments and experiences.

    C. identify and locate technology resources and evaluate them for accuracy and suitability.

    D. plan for the management of technology resources within the context of learning activities.

    E. plan strategies to manage student learning in a technology-enhanced environment.

III. Teaching, Learning, and the Curriculum

Teachers implement curriculum plans that include methods and strategies for applying technology to maximize student learning. Teachers:

A. facilitate technology-enhanced experiences that address content standards and student technology standards.

B. use technology to support learner-centered strategies that address the diverse needs of students.

C. apply technology to develop students' higher-order skills and creativity.

D. manage student learning activities in a technology-enhanced environment.

IV. Assessment and Evaluation

Teachers apply technology to facilitate a variety of effective assessment and evaluation strategies. Teachers:

A. apply technology in assessing student learning of subject matter using a variety of assessment techniques.

B. use technology resources to collect and analyze data, interpret results, and communicate findings to improve instructional practice and maximize student learning.

C. apply multiple methods of evaluation to determine students' appropriate use of technology resources for learning, communication, and productivity.

V. Productivity and Professional Practice

Teachers use technology to enhance their productivity and professional practice. Teachers:

A. use technology resources to engage in ongoing professional development and lifelong learning.

    B. continually evaluate and reflect on professional practice to make informed decisions regarding the use of technology in support of student learning.

    C. apply technology to increase productivity.

    D. use technology to communicate and collaborate with peers, parents, and the larger community in order to nurture student learning.

VI. Social, Ethical, Legal, and Human Issues

Teachers understand the social, ethical, legal, and human issues surrounding the use of technology in PK–12 schools and apply that understanding in practice. Teachers:

    A. model and teach legal and ethical practice related to technology use.

    B. apply technology resources to enable and empower learners with diverse backgrounds, characteristics, and abilities.

    C. identify and use technology resources that affirm diversity.

    D. promote safe and healthy use of technology resources.

    E. facilitate equitable access to technology resources for all students.

A

H

I

J

K

L

M

Q

R

S